"So What Are You Going to Do with That?"

"So What Are You Going to Do with That?"

Finding Careers Outside Academia

THIRD EDITION

SUSAN BASALLA AND MAGGIE DEBELIUS

The University of Chicago Press   *Chicago and London*

Susan Basalla received her PhD from Princeton University. She is a principal at Storbeck / Pimentel & Associates, LP an executive search firm specializing in higher education. **Maggie Debelius,** who also received her PhD from Princeton University, is director of faculty development and an associate teaching professor in the English Department at Georgetown University.

The University of Chicago Press, Chicago 60637
The University of Chicago Press, Ltd., London

This book was first published in 2001 by Farrar, Straus and Giroux under the title *So What Are You Going to Do with That?": A Guide to Career-Changing for MAs and PhDs.*
Third edition published 2015
Printed in the United States of America

24 23 22 21 20 19 18 17 16 15   1 2 3 4 5

ISBN-13: 978-0-226-20040-8 (paperback)
ISBN-13: 978-0-226-20037-8 (e-book)
DOI: 10.7208/chicago/9780226200378.001.0001

Library of Congress Cataloging-in-Publication Data

Basalla, Susan Elizabeth, 1970– author.
  "So what are you going to do with that?" : finding careers outside academia / Susan Basalla and Maggie Debelius. — Third edition.
    pages ; cm
  ISBN 978-0-226-20040-8 (pbk. : alk. paper) — ISBN 0-226-20040-X (pbk. : alk. paper) — ISBN 978-0-226-20037-8 (e-book) 1. Job hunting.   2.   Graduate students—Employment.   3. Career changes.   I. Debelius, Maggie, 1966– author.   II. Title.
  HF5382.7.B374 2015
  650.14—dc23
                                                          2014019937

♾ This paper meets the requirements of ANSI/NISO Z39.48-1992 (Permanence of Paper).

For my parents, with gratitude and love.
S. B.

For Mike, Charlie, and Jack, who never make me question what
I want do with my life. When I'm with them, I'm doing it.
M. D.

Contents

Preface

More than a decade after writing the first edition of this book, we believe more passionately than ever that there is a wide range of satisfying and challenging careers beyond the academy for PhDs and MAs. The job market has swung wildly since we wrote the first edition of *"So What Are You Going to Do with That?"* during the height of the Internet boom, and our second edition was released in 2007 during a serious recession. But our message remains the same: we're more interested in helping people figure out a long-term career than a short-term job. You should explore and pursue a path that will make you happy, regardless of market fluctuations.

While our message remains the same, we have made some important additions in this third edition in response to seismic changes in the graduate employment market. First, we have incorporated specific targeted advice for graduate students in the sciences, straight from those who have been there. This change reflects our increasing awareness of the intense funding and hiring challenges now facing the sciences as well as the humanities.

We've also included more advice from the growing network of university graduate career counselors. In the last decade, we've observed that while once only a few select institutions employed career counselors dedicated to helping graduate students, such positions are now increasingly common. You may know them best as the kind souls who help you transform your CV into a résumé, but they are also highly knowledgeable about the needs and preferences of individual employers as well as national hiring trends. Over the years, university career counselors have repeatedly helped us deepen our own understanding of the challenges graduate students face by sharing their advice and experiences from the front lines. We are deeply grateful for their help. And whether you're just beginning a graduate program or already finished with your dissertation, we strongly recommend making an appointment with one of these counselors.

Over the past decade we've also noticed university leaders becoming more aware of the need to address the shifting job market for graduate alumni. Ad hoc initiatives have popped up around the country and we're pleased to see these encouraging signs. However, there is much more work to be done. The number of tenure-track jobs has continued to erode at such a rate that graduate students who pursue alternatives, either inside or outside the academy, make up a new majority. We believe more strongly now than we did a decade ago that universities have an ethical obligation to help graduate students prepare for and think creatively about their options. Of course, graduate alumni are ultimately responsible for their own careers, but universities can and should do more to support their efforts.

Since publishing the first two editions of this book, we have heard from countless readers who told us that our book helped them see their talents and abilities in a new light. Some of these readers shared their stories with us and others offered suggestions for improving the next edition. We'd like to thank these readers and all the other MAs and PhDs who appear in the following pages for their generosity.

Introduction

So now what?

If you are now or have ever been a graduate student, you've heard the universal question about earning an MA or a PhD: "So what are you going do with that? Teach?" One of the occupational hazards of academic life is enduring this kind of questioning from friends and family. Your least favorite uncle has probably called you overeducated and unemployable. And maybe, somewhere in the back of your mind, you also have occasional moments of doubt about your future: What *am* I going to do with my graduate degree?

Maybe you're halfway to graduation and suddenly wondering if teaching is the right career for you. Maybe you've endured two postdocs and can't bear the thought of signing up for a third one. Maybe your heart's not in it anymore; maybe you'd like to earn more money; maybe you'd like to live somewhere where there are few college-level teaching jobs. Or maybe, like increasing numbers of graduates, you'd love to teach but can't find a tenure-track job.

Maybe you're an undergraduate feeling the path of least resistance is to move straight on into graduate school in the field of your major. With the market for college and university teaching jobs shrinking at an alarming rate, you need to consider all your options before, during, and after graduate school. Read through the stories contained here as a gut check before committing yourself to many years of graduate school. As we hear over and over again from career counselors at top universities, too many undergraduates head straight to grad school without a clear understanding of how few tenure-track jobs lie on the other side or of the debt they'll accrue along the way. We want you to have all the facts before you make the leap.

Or maybe you're a faculty member—tenured or otherwise—who's ready for a new way of life. Are you an academic nomad, traveling around the country from one adjunct position to another? Did your departmental review go badly and you just don't have the heart to seek another academic position? Or are you a tenured professor who can't face teaching the same courses and clashing with the same colleagues for one more semester? Did your spouse just land the job of her dreams at an institution not hiring in your field? This book is for faculty as well as grad students. (In fact, we were surprised in our research to see how common it was for faculty to jump ship from academia.) You'll hear advice and anecdotes from many former professors in the chapters to come.

Scientists of all stripes, we're talking to you too. Conventional wisdom says that scientists have "hard skills" and therefore don't need any help with post-academic job hunting. But we know it's not always that easy, especially if your degree is in biology or chemistry. You may have spent years enduring low pay and little autonomy as a graduate student and then as a postdoctoral fellow only to find that you're no closer to a tenure-track job. When you start to look for jobs outside academia, you may have trouble translating your experience to match employer needs. And if you want to enter an entirely new field like consulting or law, how do you prepare yourself for life outside the laboratory? We have plenty of examples and advice for you as well.

Whether you are a grad student or professor, humanist or scientist, as an academic, you may feel as if, after spending ten years studying one obscure topic, you'll never be able to reshape yourself into a real-world success. (Heck, you might not even own a suit.) We felt that way too. But, believe it or not, the same skills you need to succeed in academia—researching, writing, analyzing, and teaching—will give you the edge in your job hunt. We will suggest a number of questions to ask and strategies to employ that will help you decide whether you want to continue going to graduate school, show you how to make the best use of your time while you're there, and teach you how to market yourself to employers after you leave. We'll show you everything you need to know to translate your academic credentials into a real-world job.

We've interviewed more than a hundred former graduate students and professors who have found challenging and fulfilling careers as everything from midwife to private investigator to National Football League executive. We've also talked to people working happily in more traditional careers, such as editors, high school teachers, computer gurus, lawyers, university administrators, management consultants, entrepreneurs, and researchers. In the course of this book, we will introduce you to scores of graduate alumni from the humanities, sciences, and social sciences (and other fields as well), and explain exactly how they reached their goals. These alumni generously shared with us their advice, their anecdotes, and their secrets for success. They are all insightful, funny, inspiring, creative, and ambitious people—it was a joy to meet them. We've made their stories the heart of this book so you can learn as much from them as we did.

So Who Are We to Talk?

Since earning our PhDs, we've seen the economy in times of growth and in times of recession. We've worked our way through a variety of jobs both inside and outside the academy and have shifted our career paths along the way (more than once!) to match our evolving interests and priorities. And while we remember vividly how it feels to be a poverty- and angst-ridden grad student, we have enough distance from those days to be able to offer time-tested advice. In addition to our own experiences, we've spent the last decade listening to our readers, giving talks at universities all over the country, and working with the nation's best graduate career counselors. We've learned about your aspirations and your limitations. Whatever your circumstances, we assure you that you are not alone and that you do have options. You too can live a happy and successful life outside academia, if you are willing to do the work to make it happen.

Sue's Story: PhD in English, Princeton University, 1997

I figured out that I didn't want to be a professor about halfway through my PhD program. I realized one day that I just couldn't picture myself continuing to study the same narrow topic for the next decade. I had no idea what other kind of career would be open to me, but I knew that I wanted to finish my degree. Luckily, my adviser was supportive and agreed to help me streamline my dissertation so I could finish quickly.

Although I was worried that my parents would be disappointed by my decision to leave academia, they were actually relieved. My father (a history professor) had seen too many graduate students cycle unsuccessfully through the job market year after year and didn't want me to suffer a similar fate if I could be happy doing something else. I stocked up on Diet Coke and hummus and wrote my dissertation as fast as I could. Giving myself a deadline and knowing that I would never go on the academic job market made it much easier for me to just get it done.

During the year that I finished my dissertation, I also started researching other careers. The university career center didn't have many resources for graduate students back then (that's no longer remotely true). Hoping to find someone who understood my situation, I got a list of English PhDs from the alumni office and started cold-calling them to ask for advice. (My department chair kindly helped me get the list, though in retrospect I realize that I could have asked the alumni office for it myself.) Much to my surprise, all the alumni I spoke to seemed happy and fulfilled in their new careers and were more than willing to offer advice and contacts. Those early conversations were the germ of this book.

For the first seven years or so after finishing my PhD, I moved through a variety of positions and fields, gaining both practical experience and insight into my own strengths and preferences. I worked at a foundation, at a trade publication, at a dot-com and at a megacorporation. The path was not at all linear, but it led to my current role as an executive recruiter for colleges and universities. In my daily work, I help higher education institutions identify and recruit new leaders (presidents, vice presidents, deans, etc.) and greatly enjoy what I do. I feel that I've come full circle, bringing my interest in career narratives together with my passion for higher education. It turns out that having one foot in academia is exactly right for me. I love working with colleges and universities because I care about their mission, but I know that I can serve them better in my current role than I ever could have as a faculty member.

Maggie's Story: PhD in English, Princeton University, 2000

Throughout graduate school, I straddled the fence between the academic and post-academic worlds by working as a freelance writer. I loved teaching but struggled to find my voice as an academic writer. Journalism provided me with both a paycheck and a reminder that I could write—even when I couldn't face my dissertation. I took some time off from the dissertation to work as an editor for an Internet company in the late '90s. Like many of those we interviewed, I benefitted from taking a break from writing. My employer allowed me to work four days a week, I wrote my dissertations on Fridays and weekends, and I ended up being much more productive than when I tried to write full-time.

My own writing struggles have led me back to the academy, where I now work as Director of the Writing Center at Georgetown University in Washington, D.C. This position puts me just where I want to be: at the crossroads of the academy and the rest of the world. I teach in the English department, train the Georgetown students who staff the Writing Center, and work with writers at all stages of the composing process. I also get to work with writers who face some of the same obstacles that I faced when writing my dissertation.

I consider myself fortunate to continue to straddle the academic and post-academic divide: this position allows me to do the teaching I love and also gives me the chance to consider connections between my students' academic writing and the other writing that they do. Much of my recent scholarly work has been on the use of electronic portfolios in the writing classroom. It's exciting for me to find a format in which students can explore the connections between their curricular and extracurricular work. I also continue to work outside the academy as a writing consultant for businesses and nonprofits. The workshop techniques and editing exercises that have become staples in writing classrooms across the country have proved valuable to and effective for several companies we've worked with.

So for me the barrier between the academic and post-academic worlds continues to be a permeable one. Just as I continued to publish in academic journals while working full-time as a website editor, so I continue to work as a freelance journalist and corporate trainer while working full-time at Georgetown. Rather than feeling my life is split into two halves, I feel my interests complement each other. Working outside the academy makes me a better teacher because I can share a broad base of experience with my students (and help them job-hunt when necessary). And my academic work informs all the post-academic writing and teaching that I do, helping me adapt the best of the classroom to the workplace. Years after writing the first edition of this book, I believe more passionately than ever in the relevance of a PhD or an MA to careers outside the academy.

So What's This Book All About?

This book evolved from a series of late-night phone calls during our graduate school days in which we questioned our future prospects and self-worth. What would our friends say if we left the profession? What would our advisers think? Our parents? Our significant others? Like many graduate students who contemplate careers outside academia, we felt a little sheepish—as though, after years of academic success, we were going to fail the ultimate test: getting a tenure-track job. And even though we weren't exactly sure what we wanted for ourselves, we began researching careers outside academia. In the process, we discovered a stunning collection of smart, successful, and satisfied MAs and PhDs.

Because we'd never known such a wide range of renegade PhDs existed during our years in graduate school, we decided to collect their narratives in one place. All too often we've heard friends seeking jobs as professors announce, "I just can't imagine doing anything else." Of course they can't—many of them came straight from college and have been in grad school for the last decade. And this book is for them—to help them imagine other lives.

With that goal in mind, we're using the term "post-academic" careers instead of "non-academic" or "alternative" careers, because we want to banish the notion that there is academia . . . and then everything else. Academia is one choice among millions, although we often lose that perspective after spending years surrounded by people who've chosen identical careers.

In all our research, our most surprising discovery was that few post-academics completely abandon their academic interests. Rather, they find creative ways to continue a trajectory that started long before graduate school. Instead of making a U-turn in the middle of their lives, most of these alumni followed up on a lifelong interest or a half-forgotten talent by traveling a parallel path toward an equally fulfilling destination. Throughout this book, we will show you again and again the unexpected ways in which these alumni use their academic training in their new careers and the surprising connections between their academic interests and their post-academic careers.

So What Are We Supposed to Do Now?

The story Stacey Rees shared with us illustrates how your academic research can lead you, unexpectedly, to a post-academic career. Rees left Princeton's comparative literature PhD program after her fifth year. She now works as a nurse-midwife in New York City. Here's the tale of how and why she made that leap.

Rees wasn't making very speedy progress on her dissertation; her subject was the image of motherhood in French medieval literature. She had taken on several part-time jobs during graduate school, including one at a birthing center. She began to realize over the course of a year or two that she enjoyed her part-time job more than she enjoyed her graduate school work. She started to suspect that she was in graduate school primarily because she had been a good student as an undergraduate—a case of sheer momentum. Her part-time jobs were a way of subconsciously undercutting her own progress.

Over the next six months, she thought hard about what had been important to her before she came to graduate school, what made her happy now, and what she wanted her life to be in the future. While visiting a friend who was training to be an obstetrician and spending all day talking with her about women's health, Rees woke up that morning at 3 a.m., sat up straight in bed, and said, "I want to be a midwife!" Few of us will be blessed with that kind of epiphany (and even fewer with that *particular* epiphany), but for Rees, it was born of weeks of soul-searching about what she wanted her future to look like.

The first time an academic friend of ours heard this story, he said, "So now we're all supposed to go be midwives?" Obviously not. But his response is a great example of what we call the "Plan B" dilemma. We've all been training for exactly the same job as assistant professor, so when post-academic careers come up, the first question is "So what do *we all* do next?"—as if there can be a universal Plan B that will accommodate us all. As Rees's story shows, the decision is—and must be—highly personal.

Rees uses her graduate school skills every day. She calls herself a born teacher and knows she would miss the classroom if she gave it up completely. But as a midwife, instead of teaching undergraduates, she teaches mothers—one-on-one and in groups—at a critical point in their lives. About her research skills, she says:

Midwifery demands that you continually update your skills, and you must be able to comfortably consult, weigh, and evaluate current research. Graduate school made me comfortable with taking on the experts, so to speak. I left grad school with a tendency toward reading critically, which is especially important for supporting the practice of midwifery since it often flies in the face of conventional obstetrical wisdom.

Since leaving graduate school, she has published several academic articles, something she never did as a grad student. Rees also credits her graduate school training with two other important transferable skills. Her familiarity with academic scholarship won her a part-time editorial job with the *Journal of the American Medical Women's Association*, and her foreign-language training makes it possible for her to work abroad someday.

What we find so compelling about Rees's story is that, rather than imagining herself as "nothing but" an expert on an esoteric topic, she took from her dissertation an awareness of her lifelong interests. Instead of laboring over her dissertation and experiencing that awful "What else could I possibly do?" postpartum depression, Rees turned that process inside out. Her dissertation on motherhood gave birth to a midwife.

As every graduate student knows, your dissertation topic is a mini-Rorschach test of your personality. It's great cocktail party conversation to psychoanalyze people based on their choice to study, say, Marilyn Monroe rather than Emily Dickinson. But in order to imagine a life outside academia, you'll need to open up that process, as Rees did, and figure out what your dissertation, and your graduate school experience as a whole, has taught you about yourself.

Another reason we like Rees's story is that it explodes some of the most prevalent myths about post-academic careers. The myths about what graduate students can and can't do, what employers do and don't want, are extremely powerful. Debunking these myths is one of our major reasons for writing a career guide just for academics. As one former economics grad student cited in a *Chronicle of Higher Education* article put it: "Graduate school is the academic equivalent of Parris Island. The fact that . . . boot camp demoralizes you does not mean you are not capable." We went through the same basic training and can tell you that shaking that mind-set is the most important step you can take toward a satisfying life outside academia. Undoing this conditioning is hard work, but if you believe that you have somehow failed your higher purpose, you will never be happy outside academia, no matter what job you find.

You are almost certainly undervaluing yourself, right now, this very minute, as you read this book. Listen to what Victoria Blodgett, Director of Graduate Career Services at Yale University, says about you: "I want to tell graduate students how amazing they are. From this side of the desk, it is crushing to hear them say 'I have no skills. I can't do anything.' It is crushing to hear that our most accomplished, most interesting, most intellectually vigorous people feel that they have nothing to offer the world." Blodgett advises hundreds of graduate students every year and she has seen over and over again the remarkable transformation that you and all your peers are capable of making.

Yet, the fear of failure is difficult to overcome. For Sharyl Nass, a PhD in cell and tumor biology, it was one of the biggest barriers to exploring jobs outside the academy. For her, contemplating the transition was "agonizing" because "my scientific mentors told me I was throwing my career away" by leaving the academy. "There is incredible bias and arrogance in academia with regard to 'alternate' careers in science," she explains. But since finishing a postdoctoral fellowship at Johns Hopkins University and moving to a health policy position at the Institute of Medicine, she has found real satisfaction rather than imagined failure. She now uses her knowledge to advise the White House on issues surrounding cancer treatment and prevention.

Another scientist, Shannon Mrksich, recalls explaining to her parents that she wouldn't be wasting her doctorate in chemistry by becoming a patent attorney. "Helping resolve biotechnology patent disputes is another way of helping to cure cancer," she remembers telling them. "People always say, 'You've spent your whole life doing this, and now you're throwing it all away,'" Mrksich says. "But they never think to say, 'What a great stepping-stone to other things.'"

So What Can Universities Do?

Since we published the first edition of this book a decade ago, prospects for employment in higher education have dropped precipitously. Perversely, the number of tenure-track jobs has continued to decline while the number of PhDs awarded has continued to grow. At this point, tenure and tenure-line faculty make up less than 25 percent of all college teachers.

We hope undergraduates will consider the facts before applying to graduate school. And while most of us heard similar horror stories back when we applied to graduate school ourselves, we thought that we might be one of the lucky ones. But with diminishing endowments and dwindling higher-education budgets, it's clear that this employment crisis is far from temporary and the decline in tenure-track positions is unlikely to reverse itself.

The shortage of tenure-track faculty positions has led to considerable anger and frustration among graduate students. Their anger at PhD underemployment has been directed at professional associations, university administrators, and other similar targets. Many universities and professional associations have responded to the job shortage, and great strides have been made in addressing this crisis since we first began writing about this topic more than a decade ago. We've seen enormous growth in the number of universities with dedicated career counselors for graduate students and a greater willingness among university administrators to admit that the job crisis makes "alternative" careers for some PhDs a necessity.

From our perspective, the next frontier is the academic department. As Bev Ehrich, a career adviser at Brown University, notes, many "faculty don't understand and/or don't support career development beyond training for a faculty position." What will it take for faculty to acknowledge how different the academic market is today from the one in which they were hired? We offer some suggestions for how departments can help below:

• Track and assess the careers of all PhDs and MAs—not just for one to two years after degree completion and not just for

those who enter academia. Instead track all who enter the program at one, five and ten years out. The findings are sure to be
surprising. We have found anecdotally that many a PhD steps
off the academic path after a year or two as an adjunct, but
their home department still counts them in the "academic"
column.

- Maintain a database or social network of graduate alumni employed outside the academy who are willing to talk to students
about their career choices on an informal, ad hoc basis, over
phone or e-mail. Some departments have already begun con-
vening an advisory panel of graduate alumni who can share a
real-world perspective on alternative careers. Ideally, a graduate student could be given a stipend to manage and update the
database each year.

- Pool resources with other departments rather than creating
programming or alumni databases for each individual department. The differences between disciplines are far less important outside academia, and students will benefit from seeing a
wider range of options. All the humanities departments could
join forces, for example, and have much greater impact with
less wasteful duplication of effort.

- Create policies and opportunities that encourage students
to explore subjects and develop skills beyond those narrowly
considered to be necessary. Allowing students to use their
summers to do an internship or take a class that has no direct
bearing on their dissertation can help them find work more
quickly after graduation and enrich their value on the academic market at the same time.

Even if a department is already taking the above steps, they
may well undercut their own efforts through silent (and sometimes quite vocal) disapproval of post-academic careers. Real
progress requires a shift in attitude. Too many graduate students
hide their post-academic career searches from their advisers and
dissertation committees for fear of being unjustly labeled failures.
Shaming a student into an unwanted (and often unattainable)
academic career helps no one. But to be fair, we've also heard

from sympathetic and supportive faculty who say they are silent because they just aren't sure how to be helpful when it comes to post-academic careers. These faculty have told us that they worry that simply raising the topic might be misinterpreted as a suggestion that the student lacks the intellectual heft for an academic career. They're also afraid that they have little useful advice to offer since they have never been in the "outside world" themselves. We hope graduate students will bear in mind these comments and feel empowered to raise the topic themselves. If you are worried about your adviser's reaction, just share the worrying statistics about the job market and ask, "What do you think about these numbers? How can we best prepare for the possibility that there may never be a tenure-track job out there for me, no matter how hard I work?"

And What Can You Do?

While universities need to make changes, those changes won't happen quickly enough to improve your prospects if you are a grad student or professor today. Without absolving universities of responsibility, we believe that it is counterproductive to rage against a deeply rooted problem while accumulating enormous personal debt, both literally and figuratively.

We're not suggesting that post-academic careers are the magic-bullet solution to the job crisis. But whatever reforms are instituted may be too late to help those who are currently living below the poverty level while adjuncting at multiple institutions. We're here to say that you have a choice. If you decide that you want or need to leave academia for economic, geographical, family, or other reasons, we can help you figure out another path to happiness, security, and intellectual fulfillment.

Not a single person we interviewed regretted leaving academia. While some acknowledged missing certain aspects of academic life, they found compensatory virtues in their post-academic careers. A few alums who deeply loved teaching told us that they would consider returning to some kind of college-level teaching again in the future, but only on their own terms—as one option among many other jobs, or perhaps as a part-time pursuit—and not with the kind of desperation that a rookie academic brings to the job market.

We recognize that our enthusiasm about post-academic careers could be mistaken for naive optimism. Critics of "alternative" careers have remarked that graduate students who have spent years preparing to be scholars don't want to settle for boring office jobs. But your fate is in your hands. If you want interesting work, you must devote yourself to finding it. If you think that you can't possibly be happy outside academia, you probably won't be.

We understand that academia is a way of life—we felt the pain of leaving the fold—but believe us, the pain does not last. We understand that being forced to leave a career you love because of a weak job market is heartbreaking. But does that mean you should continue miserably treading water?

Let's look at your options. What are you supposed to do if you don't get a job the moment that you finish your degree or postdoc? You're supposed to take a one-year teaching job or sign on for yet another postdoc in order to patch together an income—and if you're lucky, some health insurance—while you wait for your next shot at a tenure-track position. But we all know the sad truth is that the longer you spend adjuncting, the less likely you are to land that rare tenure-track job. And in the sciences, one postdoc may just lead to another, and you may quickly find yourself having been a postdoc longer than you were a graduate student. You may become unfairly marked as undesirable. And sadly, it's often the most devoted teachers and scholars who are willing to endure low pay and crummy working conditions the longest in hope of winning the tenure-track lottery.

So here's our radical proposal: Why not get a post-academic job while you wait for next year's market? You can shrink the pool of willing adjunct teachers and postdoctoral fellows. You can earn twice as much money at a job that doesn't consume your life the way academia does. You can live where you want to live—maybe even in the same state as your spouse or partner. You can work nine to five and use your free time to teach a class on the side if you like. You can start knocking down your mounting credit card debt, prepare yourself for another career, and take back some power for yourself. When the hiring season starts again, you may decide that you're happy where you are. And if you do decide to go back on the market, it'll be on your own terms. You'll be a stronger and more confident candidate for having proven yourself in the outside world—plus, you won't feel pressured to take any academic job that's offered.

Yes, we know it's not that easy and that there are serious risks in walking away from the "pure" academic track. But we propose that you consider the possibility—even if just for a moment—as an alternative to spending yet another year as an adjunct. In the face of so much despair about what PhDs can and can't do with their lives, we are willing to err on the side of optimism. We're here to say that as intimidating as the process appears at first, there is a universe of possibilities open to you. This is the beginning of a new phase in your life—a chance for you to find out something unexpected about yourself.

What You'll Find in This Book

Chapter 1—"Will I Have to Wear a Suit?"—will help you assess your current situation and gain some perspective on what a post-academic career might offer you. Figuring out what you want to do, rather than what you're supposed to do, is the crucial first step. If you're in a rut trying to finish a project for which you (or your adviser) have lost enthusiasm, we can show you how to experiment with other fields without burning bridges behind you. We will debunk a few myths about post-academic careers and share advice from alums who've been there. We'll also address some of the psychological baggage that comes with the decision to explore careers outside the academy. Finally, this chapter will show you how to make the best use of your grad school years by gaining new kinds of experiences on and off campus.

Chapter 2—"How Do I Figure Out What Else to Do?"—will introduce you to some self-evaluation exercises designed especially for graduate students. Before you start career shopping, you have to develop a general idea of what kind of career suits you best. Aimlessly trying on labels like "systems analyst," "pastry chef," or "hotshot lawyer" will only end up frustrating you if you don't know what your own limits are. The chapter ends with an overview of the industries to which academics seem drawn, along with profiles of alums working within those fields.

Chapter 3—"Asking the Big Questions"—will help you locate and zero in on organizations that interest you. We'll explain why sending out lots of résumés can actually reduce your chances of getting an interview and then show you step-by-step how to change your approach for better results. In addition, we'll show you how combining your graduate degree with an internship, part-time job, or volunteer work can help you leapfrog ahead of the competition.

Chapter 4—"This Might Hurt a Bit"—tackles one of the toughest obstacles facing former graduate students. Reorganizing your carefully developed curriculum vitae can be a painful experience. We'll help you figure out how to put your best foot forward without feeling like a sellout. We'll also show you résumés from real-life job seekers so you can see for yourself how they translated their academic skills into desirable commodities for an employer.

Chapter 5—"Sweaty Palms, Warm Heart"—will prepare you for those nerve-racking interviews. You only have one shot with most employers, and you need to know how to sell your skills before you set foot in their offices. What do you say about your time in academia? How do you convince them you can do a job you've never done before? We'll combine specialized alumni advice with general interviewing tips to give you the confidence you need to win the job. Then we'll suggest how to negotiate your terms.

To keep all this career hunting in perspective, in the conclusion we'll look at the bigger picture. What if you still aren't sure what you want to do? What if you hate your first job? You'll hear from academics who've had long careers outside universities and can offer some important advice.

It's gut-wrenching to change careers. It takes chutzpah. But it can also turn out to be the best thing you've ever done.

1 Will I Have to Wear a Suit?

Rethinking Life After Graduate School

Hearing that there is a universe of post-academic careers open to you can be more intimidating than reassuring. Following the academic track into an assistant professorship at least offers the comfort of a clearly defined path and plenty of fellow travelers. But if you venture outside academia, you are on your own. You may not even know anyone who works in the "real world." How are you supposed to decide where you belong?

While people in all kinds of professions wish for a clearer view of the career path ahead, graduate students and faculty members face some obstacles particular to academia. There's peer pressure from other academics, who think that leaving the profession means "failure"; there's personal and family angst over the large amount of time and money you've spent earning an advanced degree; and there's an annual job market that means long waits between job-hunting attempts. Whether you're 100 percent or only 10 percent sure that you should be in academia, taking a little time to explore what else is out there will help ensure that your choice is informed by desire, not habit or tradition.

We don't want to talk you out of an academic career—it may be exactly the right choice for you, and the professorial life has some wonderful benefits. But because there are few voices out there to support those who are a little unsure, a little curious, or just plain stuck, we want to be your guides to exploring other possibilities.

You might accuse us of glamorizing life outside academia. But, hey, we've lived there—we know perfectly well that some days are miserable, some bosses are unbearable, and some jobs are just plain awful. But instead of emphasizing the negative, we've chosen to tell you about people who've worked their way through a maze of sometimes boring, usually low-level jobs to land in careers that are just right for them. And if we tell you about people who've succeeded against long odds, then it should be all the easier for you to picture yourself landing a "not perfect but a step in the right direction" kind of job.

Whatever you decide to do with your future, we want you to make a conscious choice. Former Columbia University English professor John Romano points out that while academic careers are considered to be the "safe" road to take after graduate school, the traditional approach carries more consequences than most PhDs realize. "Following tradition and taking that job at a small college in rural Nebraska is as risky as anything you do outside academia," he explains. In his own career, Romano turned down a job at a well-respected university because he feared its rural,

---

HOW CAN I EXPLORE OTHER CAREERS WHEN MY PRINCIPAL INVESTIGATOR OWNS MY TIME?

Every time we give a talk on campus, we inevitably hear from one of the biology or chemistry grad students in the audience: "You say that we should take a few hours a week to explore other careers, but that's impossible for me. My principal investigator (PI) is my employer and he owns all my time." We turned to Samantha Sutton to address this myth. Sutton earned her PhD in neurobiology from MIT and then decided to put her skills to work as a life coach for the Handel Group, where she works with graduate students, postdocs, and principal investigators at places like Stanford, MIT, the National Cancer Institute, and the Scripps Research Institute. Here's her response to this perennial complaint:

Every grad student claims that the PI is policing the lab. They don't. I talk to PIs all the time. They are so busy, they have no time to police the lab. They are giving talks, teaching, traveling, serving on search committees. How often do you even see the PI in the lab? It's a myth, like alligators living in the sewer. Everyone says, "No, mine really checks that we're there," but they don't. Try it—stay home sick one morning. Does the PI notice? When you sign up for grad school, you really aren't committing to every waking hour in the lab.

Still not convinced? Alice Ly, former Associate Director of Postdoctoral Affairs at Yale and a developmental neurobiology PhD, agrees that your PI is not paying as much attention to you as you might think. She discovered that once she told her PI that she was thinking about careers outside academia, her PI offered to help her network with contacts at pharmaceutical companies. But yes, some PIs are more reasonable than others. Ly advises testing the waters with your PI by, for example, mentioning that you're thinking of attending an upcoming talk about post-academic careers and seeing how he or she responds. Ly also suggests thinking of your evenings as your personal time to explore other activities, whether personal or professional, to help you figure out your strengths and interests outside the lab.

Ultimately, however, it's up to you. "It all depends on how motivated you are," says Shaohua Zhou, a consultant for Gallup Consulting who earned his PhD in developmental and cell biology at University of California–Irvine. "Nobody ever has enough time. It's true whoever you are. Nobody does. If you want something, you sleep less." Zhou is living proof of what can be accomplished during graduate school as he launched several start-up companies while earning his degree. It took him longer to finish his doctorate, he acknowledges, but the tradeoff was intentional because he knew that he wanted to build up his entrepreneurial experience along the way. No matter what your goals are, the excuse of not having enough time just doesn't hold up, according to all the scientists we interviewed. If you want to find the time, you can do so, but the decision is yours.

small-town environment would cut off his escape routes to other careers. Romano advises current academics to remember that "it's too easy to drift into academia, but at the same time, drifting into it is also making a choice. . . . The fact that you are good at one thing doesn't mean you have to do it for the rest of your life. You may be good at other things, too, and never know it."

Romano himself took a big chance when he decided to leave Columbia to try a screenwriting career in Hollywood. Instead of writing the book that he needed to get tenure, Romano wrote a screenplay and began sending it out to movie studios. While the move was risky both personally (he had a wife and young child) and professionally, Romano's gamble paid off; he made it to Hollywood, where he's written for both movies and television. He credits Charles Dickens—the subject of his dissertation—with helping him understand how to write the modern version of popular serial fiction. Some of his career highlights include writing and producing such shows as *Hill Street Blues*, *Party of Five*, and *Monk*.

Getting Your Head Ready

We've given talks to graduate students at a dozens of universities since this book was first published, and in doing so we've learned that the greatest obstacle to a PhD's employment outside academia lies inside his or her own head. The emotional and psychological issues that leaving academia conjures up for most graduate students are a far greater barrier than employer indifference or lack of relevant skills. Leo Simonetta, a PhD in social psychology and former faculty member who now works outside the academy in survey research, explains that the very nature of academia makes leaving difficult. First, the path from graduate school to a professorship seems clear, but the tight job market means only a few PhDs will reach that destination, which is extremely frustrating. Second, many graduate students fear that searching for a post-academic job is a tacit admission that their years in graduate school have been wasted. And finally, Simonetta notes, academics tend to stereotype those who work outside the academy as greedy and materialistic, making a difficult decision even harder for those contemplating a change of career.

Another major concern for graduate students is a fear of losing one's identity. An anthropology graduate student from the University of Michigan, Karen Rignall, describes herself as "terrified and tormented" at the thought of leaving her program:

> I was afraid that I was quitting, that I was weak, that I couldn't finish anything. I loved Morocco and feared that I'd be giving up my relation to the place since I was supposed to do my fieldwork there next year. I was studying for generals at the time, and feared that I was copping out. I'd built my identity around these books I'd read, these people I know, and I thought that no one else would understand me—I'm unique. I worried that I would no longer know what the newest development in theory is, and I wouldn't be able to talk to anyone.

Rignall's fears were not realized. After a year outside academia, "I got over my elitist sensibility and learned that I don't have to talk through theory books to relate to someone," she says.

A former graduate student in philosophy, John DeSanto, worried that he didn't have the skills to get a post-academic job. Combining his story with Rignall's illustrates how graduate school teaches us simultaneously to overestimate and underestimate our abilities. As DeSanto sees it: "You get used to feeling like a nothing in grad school. You don't realize you could do more. A friend who left my department two years before I did tried to tell me that it was okay to leave, but I just didn't hear her." DeSanto left his program to work for Cycorp, a Texas-based artificial intelligence company founded by a former philosophy professor and staffed by dozens of former philosophy grad students. Happy in his new career, he found that "I talk about philosophy at work these days more than I ever did in grad school."

For others, the decision to leave academia revolves around less dramatic, but no less painful, questions about trading quality of life for a long shot at a tenure-track job. Anne-Marie Cziko was only two years into her neuroscience PhD program at the University of Arizona when she began having serious doubts about pursuing a tenure-track position. "I started meeting people who were on their second or third postdoc. That worried me. And then I met a postdoc who was so brilliant—he lived and breathed science—and had several publications but struggled to land a job. And then when he finally did get a tenure-track job, he lost his funding a few years later." Cziko decided to finish her degree even though she knew she wouldn't become an academic: "I love science but I wasn't sure that I wanted to give up everything for it." Cziko ultimately created her own position with a Los Angeles nonprofit focused on K-12 education by offering to help them incorporate basic principles of neuroscience into their enrichment programs.

Faculty members who decide to leave tenure-track or tenured positions for post-academic careers face a different set of concerns than grad students, of course, but many of the emotions are similar. Alexandra Lord, a British history PhD, found a tenure-track job with an ideal two-two teaching load at Montana State University soon after finishing her dissertation. Although she was lucky to find a job in her field, she went on the market again immediately as the isolation of living in Bozeman (made worse by the fact that she did not earn enough to afford a car) caused her to question whether the sacrifices academia required were worth the rewards: "Gradually, I realized that I had given up all the things which had made me want to be a historian (museums, bookstores, archives, theater, etc.) simply so that I could be a professor teaching kids who were, at best, only marginally interested in British history." Lord, who now works as a historian for the National Park Service, says, "I should have acknowledged that I didn't like academia earlier, and I should never have listened to people who told me that only losers leave academia."

Whether you are a faculty member or a graduate student, some of your concerns are unique to academia, but others are common to most working adults. Absolutely everyone has to make trade-offs when they accept a job. Maybe the hours are too long but the pay is good. Maybe the commute is short, but the work is not that interesting. Maybe the work is wonderfully satisfying but pays too little. And once you think you've got it all figured out, you have to do it all over again because your much-beloved boss has been replaced by a hard-headed tyrant and now your dream job is a nightmare. Ultimately, we can't give you any simple answers on how to avoid having to revisit these big life questions from time to time, because we haven't figured the final answer for ourselves (and neither has anyone else).

As John Romano told us, academics who ask him for career advice "seem to want answers as institutionalized and direct as academic life. But the world isn't that clear-cut. You must improvise." Alice Ly, who advised doctoral students and postdoctoral fellows in her role as Associate Director of Postdoctoral Affairs at Yale, agrees. "Science students need to sit down and derive their own answers based on their own wants and needs, not on external factors like what others are doing, or what is expected of them," she said. Graduate students often wanted her to tell them what to do with their lives, but she would say, "I can't decide for you. While you might not know all the possibilities that are out there for you yet, you do know what you like and what you don't like, what you do well and what you don't do well." Ultimately, whatever your field or stage of career, these life decisions are deeply personal. It's your life, and only you can decide how to live it.

Should I Finish My Dissertation?

Among the many fears that can keep a distressed graduate student in the humanities or social sciences awake at night, the biggest one is usually: Should I finish my dissertation or not? (And sometimes the question emerges even earlier: Should I quit before even starting my dissertation?)

Sean Boocock struggled with the question of whether to finish after completing a year in the philosophy doctoral program at Notre Dame. It slowly dawned on him that he didn't want to spend the rest of his life in academia, and the realization was traumatic. "For most of my life I had identified with a tenure-track academic career. I was so focused on the academic career path that I had lost sight of possible alternatives after graduate training, and more importantly what made me happy; there was always the next rung of the academic ladder to focus on," he recalls.

He learned that philosophy was not what he thought of every morning when he woke up, that it wasn't what motivated him. He had a "growing realization that school felt more like an obligation" than a satisfying endeavor, he explains. Eventually he left Notre Dame for an MA program in Computer Science at the University of Southern California where he focused on video game design. He has since launched a successful career as a game designer with Electronic Arts and looks back on leaving his doctoral program without regret.

While we can't tell you the right answer about whether to finish your degree, we can tell you that you don't have to torture yourself by trying to decide on an absolute "yes" or "no." Instead, concentrate on taking control of your progress in the short term. This may sound like we're calling for some sort of grad student revolt; we're not. We're just trying to correct the over-inflated idea most grad students have of their adviser's investment in their progress. Admit it: you've probably had nightmares in which your adviser has wreaked Godzilla-like havoc on your tiny studio apartment. As a young civil engineering professor told us: "It was a surprise to me when I became a professor to see how wrong I was about my adviser's level of interest in me. I wish my grad students well, but I don't stay up at night worrying about them or calculating how fast they're working."

Many graduate students we interviewed talked about feeling held captive by a slow-moving or indecisive adviser. One humanities student described how his adviser's behavior caused him to leave his program A.B.D. ("all but dissertation" completed). Although the grad student was writing steadily, his adviser took a year to read each chapter he produced and then things got even worse:

After two years of work on my dissertation in one direction, my advisers pulled the rug out from under me. If graduate school were a company and they were managers, they would've been fired long ago. I was in my seventh year—it was awful. When they told me I was going to have to start over, I thought, "I'm going to have a nervous breakdown and I don't even have health insurance."

Based on his experience, he advises other grad students to beware of "letting sluggish advisers pull you off track." If he did it all over again, he says, "I'd be smarter about it, tougher about it. I'd treat grad school more like a job—work nine to five and meet my adviser with some pages every Friday."

Maybe such time-clock discipline is unrealistic for you. The key here is to unfold that road map for yourself and not let your adviser do all the navigating. Asserting yourself may cause a little friction, but in general your adviser does not have as much interest in you, or power over you, as you imagine. For example, one professor confided to us that she feels relieved whenever one of her grad students announces that she or he won't be going on the market for the third or fourth time. "It's a tough market," she acknowledges, "and I'm glad that they have decided to escape the cycle."

And ultimately, your life is your own. As Katja Zelljadt, a PhD in history who now works as associate director of the Stanford Humanities Center, puts it: "At 30 years old, you're an adult in any other context. It's frightening to me how infantilized graduate students can become. It's your life and you have to make yourself happy. It's remarkable how hard it is for some people to come to the realization that they don't have to live their lives to please their adviser. If you feel you don't have control over your life, then that is the issue you need to address."

Whether you are just beginning to question your future as an academic or nearing the end of your proverbial rope, understand that you do have options. Here are some approaches that different alumni have used to get out of their grad school ruts:

Speak frankly with your adviser about your job market concerns, your financial and family pressures, and your personal happiness. Think about how you would like the next few years of your life to look. Is it time to move on? Do you need more financial stability? Is your spouse/partner/parent/beloved pet running out of patience with you? Are you tired of sacrificing the present for an uncertain future? What is the outlook for hiring in your field? Have you talked to your adviser about the realistic odds of your getting a tenure-track job? Consider telling your adviser you'd like to work together to set a schedule for finishing your dissertation by a certain date. While you might think that an adviser would be horrified by such a pragmatic approach, you'll probably be surprised. Your adviser will likely be pleased that you are taking ownership of your project.

Once you've broken the ice with your adviser, you can also talk about modifying your project. If your discipline allows, writing a shorter, more focused dissertation (as opposed to one that is halfway to becoming an academic publication and primed for the job market) will allow you to earn your degree, but also get on with your life. As far as the world outside the academy is concerned, there are two kinds of dissertations: finished and unfinished.

Take a few months off. If just thinking about your project makes you feel hopeless and miserable, step back and get some perspective. You don't need to make any big decisions yet. Take an intensive language course abroad. Do a formal or informal internship (see chapter 3 for more advice on this topic). Get out of your head and off your campus, whether by taking a formal leave of absence or a self-imposed sabbatical. You'll earn some money, gain some experience, and maybe even clarify your desire to be an academic. Over and over again, alumni have told us that once the dissertation was no longer the looming presence in their lives, they found it much easier to just write the damn thing. Other alumni decided after taking a break that finishing their dissertation simply wasn't worth it. Both are valid conclusions. And if a few months off isn't practical for you or your challenge isn't about writing but rather time in the lab, give yourself at least one day, two days, or a week off. Shut down your e-mail, turn off your phone, and run away. Do something you've always wanted to do, something that feels wildly indulgent, something totally unrelated to your academic work—and see how you feel after a mental break.

Decide that you sure as hell will finish this stupid thing . . . but

not right now. Promise yourself that you'll finish your dissertation eventually, and then give yourself permission to pack it up into a box for the present. Rodney Whitlock, a political science PhD who finished his dissertation three years into his new job on Capitol Hill, told us: "I always said that I could finish it in two months, but I just never did it before. At the time I left academia, there were no jobs, so there was no incentive to finish." By stint of sheer will and several trips to Office Depot for legal pads and exactly the right kind of pen, Whitlock got it done in two months, just as he'd predicted. Leaving open the question of when to finish will free you to explore other interests. Come back to your dissertation in a few months, or a few years.

Or you can just let it go. Maybe the topic just doesn't thrill you anymore; maybe the field is getting overcrowded; maybe your project has had so many setbacks it just seems doomed. Make your peace with it. Grad-student-turned-career-expert Nick Corcodilos described his reason for leaving Stanford's cognitive psychology program A.B.D. as frustration over a lack of intellectual independence. He wanted to do his own research, not his adviser's, and has no regrets about leaving academia. If you are more ambivalent than Corcodilos, remember that the average person (not to mention most of your relatives) thinks writing a dissertation or completing a PhD is odd in the first place. About 99 percent of the population manages to get through life sans PhD, and we are confident that you can too.

Or decide not to decide. There's nothing wrong with hedging your bets. If you're ambivalent about leaving academia, straddle the tracks for a while. Pursue both options simultaneously, and make the big decisions only when forced. The boundary between academia and the post-academic world is more permeable than you may realize.

How to Use Your Grad School Years Wisely

You're going to spend at least four or five years in graduate school. The national average is closer to a decade. What will you have to show for yourself besides teaching and research? We beg you to pursue some other interest, any other interest, during these years for three important reasons. First, having other interests will help you manage your stress and keep your academic endeavors in perspective. Second, you'll actually make faster progress on your academic work, believe it or not, when it is not the sole, looming presence in your life. And finally, no matter what other interest you pursue, however frivolous it may seem, you will expand your future career options by adding new skills and experiences to your repertoire.

In chapter 3 we'll talk about deploying volunteering, part-time work, internships and other kinds of hands-on experience as an intentional, targeted strategy for gaining experience or test-driving a particular career, but in this chapter we're talking about something quite different. We're saying that you should keep on being a part-time DJ or teaching karate classes or riding horses or spending your summers working in a family business or climbing mountains or tutoring kids or just earning some extra spending money through any kind of part-time work. You pick the activity, no rules here, but please, do something utterly unrelated to your academic work. Use a different side of your brain, stretch a different set of muscles. Don't worry about whether it seems like this activity could be your Plan B career or not—just do what you love. No matter what you think you might do after graduation, it is too great a risk, both personally and professionally, to devote yourself solely to academia when the job prospects are so dim. Keep pursuing your passions, your hobbies, your interests beyond academia so that your options remain open and your head stays clear. And if you are lucky enough to land a tenure-track job, then you'll emerge from graduate school as a happy and well-rounded faculty member—you can't lose.

We want to tell you a story that beautifully illustrates the reasons we list above for pursuing other interests while you're in grad school. Michelle Squiteri was trying to finish her dissertation on medieval and Renaissance love lyrics at the University of California–Berkeley, and took a job as a secretary at a private investigation firm to earn extra money. She wasn't thinking at the time that she needed a backup plan, but "maybe I had an

GRAD SCHOOL TIME VS. POST-ACADEMIC TIME

Many of the alumni we interviewed noted that the pace of daily life altered dramatically once they entered the professional world. "One day in the business world is equivalent to about three weeks in academia," history PhD turned McKinsey management and financial consultant Emily Hill estimates.

Depending on where you work, your typical day might change significantly after you enter the workforce. But those changes are not necessarily for the worse, as Hill describes:

> I used to work all day and accomplish so little—now I get much more done, and without all the procrastination. I go home knowing I've done a good day's work, instead of feeling guilty all the time. I miss drinking coffee in my bathrobe at 11 a.m., but in a way, I also hated myself then for not getting enough done. I worked inefficiently, never felt like I'd accomplished anything. If I do go back to academia, and I may someday, I will be ten times more productive than if I had stayed.

Other alumni, such as Rodney Whitlock, a political science PhD who now burns the midnight oil working on Capitol Hill, recalls similar grad school frustrations. "I hated the feeling that you were never really busy, and never really not busy. I hated the nagging feeling over the weekends," Whitlock remembers.

The faster pace of post-academic jobs means that the standard for quality work is quite different as well. Steve Sampson, a doctoral student whose first job was writing for a tech company, learned in the initial months on the job that "the goal is not so much to get things absolutely 'right' as it is to get things done 'as well as possible' in a brief amount of time."

eye out, knowing that I needed an alternative to academia," she said. "The investigators were doing research in public records, interviewing people, and writing reports—it seemed similar to what I was doing." While it was "painful to realize I had to go back to square one," Squiteri calls her secretarial job "one of the best things I did."

For a year and a half, she worked at the PI firm while producing chapters of her dissertation more quickly and steadily than she had in years: "When I got into work that was professional and interesting, I just felt better about myself. I knew that I could finish my dissertation then. I set a deadline and kept it." The perspective she gained from working outside academia made the dissertation seem like a manageable task, rather than the end-all, be-all of her existence.

The other important benefit of her job was that it opened her eyes to another possible career: "When I saw what the investigators did, I knew that I liked it, and I knew that I could do it." After learning the ropes as a secretary, Squiteri sought advice on how to make the leap to investigator. She arranged an information interview with a well-known criminal investigator. During the meeting, Squiteri explained what she'd learned in the PI office and why her academic skills would be useful in investigative work: "I told him that sonnets are full of deliberate vagueness and hinting: readers have to unravel the mystery, find the clues. In *The Hound of the Baskervilles,* Sherlock Holmes tucks a volume of Petrarch's poetry in his pocket on his way to work on a case. It's perfect!" Her contact suggested she start by looking for a job in civil investigation, such as insurance fraud work, to learn the skills of the trade and then move up into criminal work. She followed his advice and now works as a full-time criminal investigator in a job that she enjoys enormously but that also leaves her "energy and time for myself."

While working as an investigator, Squiteri gave the academic market one more try: "Already having a job as an investigator made the academic job market less stressful. I felt much more secure and much less desperate. My husband decided he was going to teach no matter what the price, but I felt insecure and horrified by the idea of having a degree and being on my own as a teacher." In the end, she was offered a tenure-track job at a Midwestern university, but she turned it down. Knowing that she already had a lucrative, satisfying job that would allow her to stay in the Bay Area she loved made the choice much easier.

She has not abandoned all things academic, however. Squiteri spent six months teaching in France and published an article in a

THE HIDDEN VALUE OF MENIAL OFFICE WORK

No one with an advanced degree should waste his or her time in a low-level office job, right? Well, even in the most PhD friendly workplaces, employers want to see evidence you've got some basic office skills, warns John Rumm, a PhD who worked with History Associates in Rockville, Maryland.

"If we're looking at two résumés from graduate students, and one has worked in an office job and one has never set foot outside academia, we're going to take the one who's worked in an office before. It doesn't matter if it's a low-level job or unrelated to your interest," Rumm says.

Why is office experience so important? Because it shows that you can work with other people in addition to performing certain basic tasks, like making a business call or writing a professional e-mail. "That way we know the person we hire won't be walking around the office starry-eyed."

So should you run out and join the secretarial pool? No. But you're likely to have done some office work along the way in a part-time job or as a volunteer. Without even realizing it, you may have gained experience that you can use to convince an employer that you're right for the job.

French academic journal. She would like to publish her dissertation and plans to return to France to teach every few years. The flexibility of investigative work allows her to pursue her intellectual interests without having to compromise her quality of life.

So What Am *I* Going to Do?

While it looks like Squiteri hedged her bets expertly and even managed to pull down an academic job offer in a tough job market, she freely admits that she had no grand master plan for her life. Most people's careers have some logical continuity to them in retrospect, but it's rare to find someone who claims to have known in advance what they would love or hate about Job A, and how that experience would prompt them toward Job B and then Job C. We found that in interviewing the enormous range of people for this book, the number one answer to the question, "How did you get where you are today?" was "Serendipity."

So what good does that do you? Well, it takes the pressure off. You're not psychic; you can't possibly predict all the moves ahead. Be open to unexpected possibilities and follow your instincts. If a job or volunteer project or hobby makes you enormously happy, run with it. A career may well develop out of it in some unexpected way, if you want it to. And if it doesn't, you'll never regret spending time on something you love. E. L. Doctorow has a great quote about writing that we think also applies to divining a career path: "It's like driving at night. Your headlights only light up the road 30 feet in front you, but that's enough to get you all the way home."

The biggest difference between academic careers and post-academic careers is that the road is almost too well-lit in academia—you don't even need your headlights. The path is excruciatingly clear. You look for a job at the same time everyone else does, and if you don't find work, you simply wait until next year to repeat the process. The free-form post-academic job market can look downright scary to someone coming from the well-ordered academic universe, so you, too, will have to reinvent your approach to job hunting for the post-academic world.

Here are a few more examples of the surprising ways that this "leap and then look" approach has paid off for other grad alumni. As you'll see, the role of these unplanned, informal, "doing it just because I want to" experiences are quite varied. For one person, the value of his/her non-academic venture was in the practical experience and personal confidence gained, for another it served as a helpful foil in a job interview, and for a third it was a test-drive for a new career.

- Karen Rignall's part-time job, which she began with the intention of maintaining her language skills, unexpectedly gave her the confidence and experience to leave the anthropology program at the University of Michigan. After her first year in grad school, she spent a year in Cairo studying Arabic and was looking for ways to keep up with the language once she returned to Michigan. "I worked part-time at an Arab community center in Detroit doing fundraising. My boss was very encouraging and kept saying that he'd hire me in a minute. That enabled me to think that I had some skills, that I could leave academia and someone would hire me." While she did step away from academia for several years to work as a fundraiser for community development organizations at home and abroad, she decided later to complete her PhD at the University of Kentucky and pursue an academic career on her own terms, having gained a much richer and deeper understanding of the communities she studies.

- Yale history PhD Emily Hill loved the outdoors, and spent a few of her summers in grad school leading backpacking trips for teenagers. Only when she was interviewing with McKinsey Consulting and needed to persuade them that she had experience working as part of a team did she realize how valuable that experience was. She was able to convince them that she was not just an "ivory tower" academic and landed the job.
- When Rodney Whitlock was a graduate student in political science at the University of Georgia, he volunteered for U.S. Representative Charlie Norwood's campaign. Much to Whitlock's surprise, Norwood invited Whitlock to join his staff after he won the election, launching Whitlock's new career on Capitol Hill.

If you're not already keeping one foot outside academia by pursuing one of your passions on the side, it's time to give yourself permission to do so. Craig Williams, a PhD in industrial psychology who sees numerous job candidates with PhDs as the Sciences Director of Employee Resources at Pfizer Pharmaceuticals, says: "Keep one foot out of academia at all times so you won't lose touch with the kinds of work offered in the business world. Don't expect your professors to understand or value your experience outside academia. Just do it anyway."

Of course we encourage you to look beyond your campus, but don't overlook the wealth of resources that are right under your nose. Here are a few ideas to get you started:

- Act in a theater production or join a singing group
- Work part-time at the art museum, the greenhouse, the development office, or any other office on campus that appeals to you
- Get to know students outside the classroom by working in residential life
- Audit a class that you have no earthly reason for taking other than that it interests you
- Get involved in advocating for causes that are important to you, whether through your own university or your professional organization

The above suggestions may not appeal to you one bit, but we hope that just by listing out a few ideas we've prompted you to think about what really would excite and reinvigorate you. Allowing yourself to focus on something other than academic work requires resisting all your social programming, but we promise that you will quickly find that it becomes its own reward.

Five Myths about Post-Academic Careers

In order to see through the fog that sometimes surrounds us in grad school, you first have to abandon some myths about post-academic careers and replace them with questions that will help you think about your skills and your potential in a more positive and productive way.

1. No one would hire me. I have no useful skills.

Academics do suffer the disadvantage of being misunderstood by most employers. Few people will recognize at a glance that your research and teaching skills can be an asset to their company. You must figure out how your experience can benefit them—the burden is on you. Try the exercises in the next chapter to help you recognize the many talents you've developed as a teacher and researcher. Also, remember that when we ask how someone's new career is similar to his or her former academic life, nine out of ten times the answer is: "I do a lot of teaching in my work." For scientists like Shaohua Zhou, a PhD in developmental and cell biology from University of California–Irvine who now works for Gallup Strategic Consulting, the scientific method is the common link between business and academia. He says that when approaching a new project as a consultant, the problem solving process is the same as when he was a graduate student: "What is the current state? What do we know? How do we break this down into smaller, manageable pieces using facts and logic?" Figure out what the analogies are in your area of interest and you'll be able to persuade others to see those same connections.

2. Your dissertation is your most valuable asset.

While it's true that you have many valuable skills, the specific content of your research is of little interest or value to most people outside academia. If you begin your job search with the idea that you are an expert on a particular topic seeking a place to ply your trade, you are likely to fail. What is valuable about your dissertation is what you learned in the process of completing it, not the product itself. Ann Kirschner, an English PhD whose career as an entrepreneur in media and technology includes the creation of satellite and internet business for the National Football League as well as Columbia University, emphasizes the value of analytical skills in today's economy: "There is simply nothing better than the liberal arts to prepare brains to accommodate the pace of today's world, where knowledge changes so quickly that you can't master any field, but can only gain the fundamentals and the ability to acquire the rest."

3. People who work in the business world are stupid and boring.

If all your friends and associates are academics, you may think this statement is true. Graduate school does forge wonderful, lasting friendships, but it also cocoons you with people who are exactly like you. Academia has its share of dull or boring folks, as does every other field. But the post-academic world offers a greater variety of backgrounds and more room for interaction than academia.

"The biggest myth that academics have about the world of business and government is that they'll be working with people who are intellectually inferior," says Howard Scheiber, a PhD in linguistics who left academia for a position as director of staff development for the New York Public Library. "This just isn't the case: there are very bright people out there, as smart as any you'll find on campus."

4. Jobs in the business world are stupid and boring.

Remember how when you were fifteen everything was boring? Shakespeare was boring, quantum physics was boring, the Grand Canyon was boring. . . . Pretty much everything was officially too dull for words. Why? Because you didn't know enough to appreciate it. But that's why you're in grad school. You got hooked once you realized that the more you learned about a topic, the more interesting it was. Treat your career exploration as another research project. Don't assume surface appearances are correct. Academic life is one of about ten million possible careers. How can you be sure that the each of the other 99.9 percent of jobs in the universe isn't for you?

5. It's too late to change careers.

In a world where layoffs and takeovers are commonplace, the job market is full of people scrambling to update their résumés, leap into different fields, or start over in midcareer. A Department of Labor survey reported that workers had an average of ten different jobs before they were forty, so there's no shame in changing tacks. The key to successful career changing is learning the customs and vocabulary of the field you want to enter and then articulating your value. "People just don't do jobs forever anymore," insists Carol Barash, a former professor who later ran her own advertising agency. "The tenure-track model of having the same job for life is outdated."

Five Questions about Graduate School and Your Future

As you read the following chapters, try to replace the myths with these questions. Focus on figuring out what you want for yourself, and don't worry about what you should or shouldn't be doing:

1. What are your assumptions about life outside academia?

How much time have you spent away from the academy? What would you miss about academic life if you left? What are your biggest fears about what might lie on the other side? How do the people around you talk about those who work outside the academy? Becoming aware of your own preconceptions is a key first step in imagining new possibilities for yourself.

2. How much experience have you had in the world outside academia?

How many people do you know who aren't academics? What do you enjoy doing aside from your intellectual work? Did you have another job before coming to graduate school? If academia truly is the only world you know, it's time to get acquainted with the other 99 percent of the universe and put your assumptions to the test.

3. Are you happy in graduate school?

Sure, "depressed graduate student" is redundant, but be honest with yourself for a moment while no one is watching. Would you like to make a change but feel you can't or don't know how? A short vacation from academia, in the form of a part-time job or volunteer project in a completely different field, could help you rediscover what you love about academia or show you an alternative path you never knew existed.

4. What are your pressing concerns? Family? Finances? The job market?

Maybe you're pretty sure that you want to be an academic but recognize that your dream may not come true. You may have a spouse/partner and children. You may be racking up enormous amounts of debt. Maybe your significant other is also an academic and you can't find jobs at the same institution. Maybe you're watching your fellow students struggle to get tenure-track jobs and worrying that it's just too much of a long shot to win one of so few openings. Keeping one foot outside academia may help you adjust more quickly, in both practical and emotional terms, if it turns out that you have to leave academia.

5. Why did you come to grad school in the first place?

Is your motivation for staying the same? Life as a professor probably looks pretty different to you now, compared to when you first mailed off that grad school application. How do your expectations match up to reality? Anna Patchias, a University of Virginia English PhD who worked part-time as a tutor during grad school and now runs her own tutoring company, recommends asking yourself these kinds of questions repeatedly throughout your grad school years: "How am I growing toward or away from the profession? What is the state of the market in my field? What would my salary be? How much debt will I have? How long will it take to pay if off?" Asking yourself these "cold-blooded questions," Patchias suggests, can help you maintain a realistic picture of what lies ahead and what the trade-offs may be.

Your Eclectic Mix

We've tried to show you throughout this chapter that there isn't a single correct path that leads to post-academic bliss. Everyone has a different story, and you'll have to make your own decisions. But one element that ties together all the options that we've presented here is what one of our interviewees calls your "eclectic mix." In other words, everyone has to discover which features of academia are most important to them, and then find some combination of activities that fulfills those needs. Your job doesn't have to be your only intellectual stimulation. In fact, some people we interviewed think of themselves as having never left academia, even though they have post-academic jobs. They simply choose to pursue only the elements of academic life that appeal to them.

Two alumni stories in particular, one from a chief executive officer of a major corporation and one from a woman who cleans houses for a living, reminded us how varied different people's eclectic mixes can be. When Robert Brawer was downsized from his job as an English professor at the University of Wisconsin–Madison in 1975, he never imagined that he'd become CEO of Maidenform, Inc. His wife's family owned the company and helped him get a start in the marketing department, but adjusting to the business world wasn't easy for him. Brawer worked his way up and learned all sides of the business, from fashion to manufacturing to finance. He's proud of having used his writing skills to improve the firm's marketing research strategy and spent a total of twenty years at Maidenform, serving as CEO from 1990 to 1995.

But Brawer remained a teacher at heart. He missed being in the classroom, so he also taught adult "great books" classes at the local library during the years he worked at Maidenform. Although his business success might seem like enough to make anyone's life complete, he recognized and addressed an unfilled need through his eclectic mix.

Louise Rafkin's search for an eclectic mix began after she left the creative writing program at the University of California–Santa Cruz. She decided that although she loved writing, "teaching American literature and composition to a gaggle of undergraduates was stressful and not very gratifying." To support herself as a writer, she began cleaning houses. She has sincere enthusiasm for a good vacuum cleaner and likes setting her own hours, but writing remains her passion. Her work has been published in the *New York Times,* the *Los Angeles Times,* and in her collection of essays, *Other People's Dirt: A Housecleaner's Curious Adventures.*

Brawer and Rafkin followed their instincts, and each ended up successful and satisfied, in entirely unexpected ways. For them, the complementary part of the equation was easy to identify. But for other people, the right ingredients for their eclectic mix are more elusive, as the following story shows. Sabrina Wenrick left an adjunct teaching position in California for a medical writing job in Washington, D.C. After she'd been in the business world for about four months, we asked her what she thought about her experience. Her answer shows that the formation of her eclectic mix will be guided by a different set of values:

> When I was teaching, I used to feel that my job was my service, my way of doing good in the world. Now I work in an office and I like what I do, but it's over at 5 p.m. and my weekends are free. So now what I need to do is decide how I want to do my service, how I want to do good in the world. And it's kind of liberating, that I can choose to do anything, that it doesn't need to be the same as what I do to earn a living.

What we love about Wenrick is the energy and creativity with which she pursues her personal eclectic mix. We hope to inspire the same kind of enthusiasm for self-discovery in you. We can't give you a road map to your post-academic career, but if you're willing to risk the first few steps, you'll discover that you already know how to find your own way.

....

POST-ACADEMIC PROFILE:
ABBY MARKOE, A.B.D. IN HISTORY OF MEDICINE,
EXECUTIVE DIRECTOR, SQUASHWISE

Exploring your career options beyond academe sounds like an awkward and time-consuming exercise, but for many people, a beloved hobby may transform unexpectedly into a perfect-fit career. Abby Markoe's story is an excellent example of this principle. While a graduate student at Johns Hopkins University, Markoe loved playing squash at her local gym. She saw the sport as an escape from the stress of her graduate program, which combined a PhD in the history of medicine with a master's degree in public health.

When Markoe played on her college's squash team as an undergraduate, she heard about squash-based urban youth education programs. After a few years in Baltimore, she began to wonder why a similar program didn't exist there as well. She and some of her fellow players co-founded Baltimore SquashWise, a nonprofit organization that provides children attending public schools in disadvantaged neighborhoods with intensive academic support and tutoring along with coaching in the sport of squash. After much soul-searching and a brief sabbatical from her graduate program, Markoe eventually decided to leave behind her academic career to become SquashWise's full-time executive director.

She notes that many of the skills she gained in academia have been helpful to her in the nonprofit world. Her experience writing academic grant applications, for example, translated beautifully to her new role and has helped her win critical funds for her organization. And her informed perspective on the issues of child health and urban poverty has enabled her to connect effectively and powerfully with donors, board members, parents, and the news media.

Markoe encourages all graduate students to find a space outside of the university where they can get away from their work, their colleagues, and their computers. Having a neutral place that allows you to sort out your thoughts on a regular basis will help you make better decisions for yourself in the long term, she advises.

SHOULD I DO ANOTHER POSTDOC?

For graduate students in the sciences, a postdoctoral fellowship used to be a brief stopover between grad school and a tenure-track position. As the number of available tenure-track positions has shrunk, more and more grad students find themselves doing two or even three postdocs in the hope that they'll be luckier on the market next time around. But is this a good strategy? How do you decide if you should commit to another postdoc if you're not successful on the job market after your first one?

For advice on this subject, we turned to Victoria Blodgett, Director of Graduate Career Services at Yale University, who advises hundreds of graduate students and postdocs in the sciences every year.

First, Blodgett says, it's important to focus on your long-term goals. Have you carefully weighed your interests, your skills, your experiences and your passions? If not, do this first. If so, then make your decision with your goals in mind. Will a second postdoc teach you a new skill, allow you to gain knowledge in an entirely new area, or otherwise give you something you didn't get from your previous experience? Did you answer yes? Then you have a great reason to do another a postdoc. For example, Blodgett shares the story of a postdoc who was passionate about collecting seashells and spent every vacation scouring beaches for new specimens. Her own academic specialty was unrelated to marine science, however, and after completing her first postdoc, she realized that she didn't want to spend the rest of her life working in that field. Her goal was to segue into a career related to the science of seashells. For her, taking on a second postdoc in a marine sciences lab would open up an entirely new path for her and move her closer to her dream.

But what if your goal is to win one of those rare tenure-track positions in biology or chemistry? Wouldn't doing a second or third postdoc be the logical way to move closer to that goal? Not necessarily. As Blodgett puts it: "I don't think a second postdoc improves your chances of getting a tenure-track job. The fact is, there is science that knocks you off your feet—there is science that is sexy and groundbreaking and people notice it. And either you are doing that kind of science or you are not. A second postdoc can't change that."

This advice may sound disheartening at first—are you just supposed to give up on having an academic career? Not necessarily. What Blodgett advocates instead is examining carefully the reasons why you have not been successful on the market to this point. Consider the following questions, for example: Where are the jobs in your field? What are those departments looking for, specifically, in their hires? Do you have the teaching skills, the language skills, and the interpersonal skills that they are seeking? If not, your best next step is to focus on addressing those challenges. After all, if you head blindly into a second postdoc without considering these questions, you could find yourself striking out on the academic market yet again, only to be held back by issues you could have addressed years earlier.

2 How Do I Figure Out What Else to Do?

Soul-Searching Before Job Searching

If you've been thinking about exploring post-academic careers, you may already have consulted some career books. Maybe you've even taken career assessments (like the Myers-Briggs Type Indicator or the Jackson Vocational Interest Survey) to figure out what jobs best suit you. Maybe you've found these exercises helpful. Or maybe you're more like Kelly Flynn, a frustrated graduate student in English who plowed through some classic career manuals only to conclude, "I don't know what color my parachute is. I think it's plaid."

Or you might be one of those people who always skips this kind of "get in touch with yourself" chapter in career books. Either you're not interested in answering a bunch of silly questions or you're already pretty sure what field you want to enter. Fair enough. You can skip ahead to chapter 3 and we won't be hurt.

But we encourage you to give our version of the "how to find yourself" chapter a quick look before you go. In addition to career exercises designed specifically for academics, this chapter also includes a special collection of a few dozen alumni profiles grouped by field (nonprofits, teaching, government) to help you narrow down your choices. We can't promise that we will identify your parachute color, but we think our alumni stories will at least spark your imagination.

You won't find any easy answers in this chapter. Unfortunately, there's no such thing when it comes to a career search. Don't let this revelation fill you with dread. In fact, embrace the ambiguity. If that task sounds daunting, just remember that none of the questions you answered in graduate school had easy answers either, so you should be right at home. Your thesis or dissertation probably posed a question so difficult that it has taken you several years to answer, right? Well, the good news is that career searches tend to go faster than dissertations.

There's no such thing as a one-size-fits-all career exploration exercise, so we've tried to design questions geared toward academics and follow up with examples of how these principles applied to other alumni. For now, we're going to ask you to take a radical step away from your library books or your laboratory rats. Devote a few hours to yourself. It's alarming to realize that many graduate students have spent more hours thinking about a conference paper than exploring their own lives. Academics are not encouraged to think about whether they enjoy what they do. Even admitting that you like teaching better than research, or vice versa, is not wise except on certain campuses where one of the two is clearly preferred. We're asking you to think about something more subtle than whether you want to work in academia. We're asking you to think about which aspects of academic life and work bring you pleasure and which parts make you miserable. Once you have that knowledge, you can not only make better decisions about what kind of academic life might suit you (a teaching-focused job with lots of committee work versus a laboratory-centered job that requires little contact with undergrads) but also about whether you may be happier in another profession altogether.

The following exercises are designed to help you identify your strengths and clarify your interests so that you can find the right career for you.

Take Inventory

We're big believers in pro and con lists. It sounds simple, but you may be surprised by what you find. Make a two-column list of everything you love and everything you hate about academia so you can view your experience more objectively.

Here's what Maggie's pro and con list looks like:

Hates	Loves
Solitude	Flexibility
Tight job market	Intellectual engagement
Humorless academic writing	Working with language
Speaking/writing to a very small audience	Sharing a love of books with colleagues
The tenure system	Mentoring students
Geographic limitations	Working in archives

And here's Sue's pro and con list:

Hates	Loves
Planning classes, grading papers	Mentoring students
Narrow, abstract research	Exploring new fields of interest
Geographic limitations	Campus life
Academic writing	Public speaking
Sitting through long seminars	Independent work
Rigid hierarchy, poor management	Funny, interesting colleagues

These are the same lists that were included in the first edition of this book, when Maggie and I both had different jobs than we have now. What's interesting is that over the years—without being conscious of it—we have both moved toward work lives that fit our list of "loves" even more closely.

The point of making a chart like this is to show that everyone experiences academia differently. Just as our lists of pros and cons differ—and we were in the same department at the same time—yours will be different from those around you. Unfortunately, most of us spend our grad school years trying to mold ourselves into the perfect job candidate and end up squashing some of those personal instincts. The point of this chapter is to remind yourself what you enjoy and what you do well, without censoring yourself.

So where do you go from here? You can let yourself be guided by one of the items on your pro list, like Robin Wagner, a medieval Chinese history PhD, did. She knew that she loved to teach but didn't enjoy the solitary research that academia required. She first applied for a management consulting job with Booz Allen Hamilton, only to find that the position required stronger quantitative skills than she had to offer. She persuaded the firm that her teaching abilities made her a perfect fit for another job—as a trainer of consultants—and was quickly hired. Wagner was able to use the skills she valued most to gain significant business experience and travel around the world.

On the other hand, you may find direction by focusing on what you don't like about university life. For example, the geographical restrictions of academic job hunting had always topped Mark Johnson's con list. After he finished up his coursework for a PhD in English at Boston University, he decided to return to his native San Diego. "The call of surfing was stronger than that of teaching anywhere at any price," he recalls. "As for a job, I reckoned I'd make one happen."

While surfing, doing freelance writing jobs, and finishing his dissertation, Johnson answered a classified ad for a technical writer at Intuit. He wasn't entirely sure what technical writing was, but he had used Intuit's Quicken software to track his (meager) finances. Between his freelance articles and his demonstrated knowledge of Intuit's products, Johnson got the job and was able to stay in the city he loved.

What if your pros and cons are more muddled than Wagner's and Johnson's? Try asking your friends and family what they've observed about you. When are you happiest? What frustrates you? Shannon Zimmerman, a University of Georgia English PhD, told us that his wife "saw what I could do when I felt very limited." She had noticed that he always started off the semester excited about teaching, but became gloomy and miserable by the end. She pointed out that he was skilled at making web pages and discussion lists for his classes and that he had always enjoyed doing journalism on the side. Couldn't those interests add up to another career? Zimmerman drew up a résumé highlighting the skills that his wife described and landed a job as a project manager with The Motley Fool personal finance website. A few years later, Zimmerman moved on to Morningstar, where he applied his new investing knowledge and his pre-existing research and writing skills as a mutual fund analyst.

Even if you're lucky enough to have a perceptive and compassionate spouse, leaving academia can be incredibly painful. Many scholars are reluctant to give up the most fulfilling parts of teaching and research, or the flexibility that goes with these activities. After having spent years in academia, you may find it hard to let go.

If you're grieving about giving up the things on your pro list, don't despair. This is really a lost-and-found exercise. You may not be able to see it from here, but over and over again alumni tell us that the intellectual stimulation or the teaching challenges that they loved in academia are big parts of their new post-academic careers as well. For example, an enormous variety of PhDs tell us their new careers—as policy wonks, management consultants, public relations executives, and computer gurus—involve some form of teaching. Just because you're not turning in grades at the end of the semester doesn't mean that you're not using your ability to mentor, instruct, and inspire.

And you may find, as Shannon Zimmerman did, that your fear of intellectual stagnation is unfounded. "I was afraid that I was leaving the world of ideas," he said, "but instead I find that I've actually entered the world of ideas."

Break It Down

This exercise can also help you avoid the common mistake of thinking that your extensive knowledge of a certain subject area is your most valuable asset. As many of the examples in this book demonstrate, the thread that leads most former academics to their post-academic jobs is not a subject matter but a skill set. Wagner didn't have to work in Chinese history to be happy; she just had to teach. Zimmerman didn't have to continue focusing on Marxist readings of the Romantic poets in order to be happy; he just needed to continue exploring the world of ideas.

Even if you can identify your pros and cons, you will probably need to be more specific than "I like teaching" or "I like researching" in order to apply that knowledge to post-academic career hunting. What exactly do you like about teaching? Is it working with students? Or public speaking? Or designing lesson plans? Breaking down your love of teaching into smaller parts can help you better understand yourself and also help you make a stronger case to an employer.

- First, think about the process of pursuing your scholarly interests, not the content of your work. List all the activities you've done: teaching, research, staff training, administration of a group or laboratory, community service, committee work, political activism, participating in professional conferences.
- Narrow down your list to the three or four activities that meant the most to you. List the tasks associated with each activity.
- Finally, write down the skills associated with each task.

Here are a few examples:

Activity: Being a teaching assistant for an upper-level art history class.

Tasks: Preparing short-term and long-term lesson plans, leading discussions, organizing visual media, managing the course website, lecturing occasionally, grading papers, settling grade disputes, mentoring students, evaluating students, working with administrators on behalf of students, writing letters of recommendation.

Transferable Skills: Organizational ability, planning and scheduling, public speaking, technical and web design skills, ability to translate complex concepts to new learners, diplomacy, interpersonal skills, supervisory skills, risk taking, interviewing.

Activity: Working in a Principal Investigator's (PI's) lab doing experiments on mice.

Tasks: Keeping accurate daily records, collecting and analyzing data, troubleshooting results, performing quantitative and statistical analyses, operating laboratory equipment, writing up results, supervising undergraduate assistants.

Transferable Skills: Attention to detail, data analysis, computer modeling, project management, complex problem solving, analytical skills, supervisory skills.

SHOULD I TEACH HIGH SCHOOL?

A PhD in American studies does not typically lead to a career in a Quaker private school, but it did for Bryan Garman. Garman worked part-time as a high school history teacher while he was on the academic job market. Over the course of a decade he transformed himself from part-time high school teacher to the head of school at Wilmington Friends, a Quaker school in Delaware. Along the way, he learned new ways of thinking about teaching, managed to turn his dissertation into a published book, and developed a deep appreciation for the Quaker way.

Q: Why did you decide to go to graduate school?

With majors in English and psychology, I had no real job prospects after college graduation. I had this vague notion that it would be fun to wear black jeans and cowboy boots and study American literature. But when I started graduate school at Emory University, I recognized that I had no idea about what I wanted to do or what being a PhD student was about.

Q: Why did you decide to leave university teaching?

I enjoyed teaching at the college level, but the job market was not great for Americanists. On my first day of graduate school, one of my advisers was brutally honest about that fact and told me to keep my eyes open for opportunities outside of the academy. For me, a career in Quaker education provided that opportunity. Having written about social movements and politically engaged artists, I was drawn to the Quaker commitments to equality and social justice. I was also intrigued by the Quakers' work in international peace initiatives and environmental stewardship. At the end of the day, the mission of Quaker education and the students I had the opportunity to teach led me to leave the academy.

Q: How did you get your first teaching job and where?

I was living in Washington, D.C., and had sent my résumé to a number of schools in the area. I was literally walking in the door from my graduation at Emory when Sidwell Friends called to see if I would be interested in interviewing for a late opening. After a few hours of conversation and a teaching demonstration, the school offered me a part-time teaching position on a one-year contract. I was told there was no possibility that my contract would be extended; I was struck that such a point had been made about that, because at that time I had no interest whatsoever in staying. The only thing I knew about the school was that the Clintons had sent their daughter there. At that point, I was still interviewing for tenure-track positions and was happy to have a part-time job while I revised my dissertation into a book.

Q: How did teaching high school students differ from teaching college students?

The adjustment was not as difficult as it might seem.

Friends school students are a highly talented, highly motivated group. They work hard, they engage ideas, and they are encouraged to take intellectual risks and think critically. There are small matters that you may need to remind them about—you may need to talk about basic study skills to tell them to take notes—and you will need to present material at a developmentally appropriate level.

Even more important, you are expected to invest yourself in the total development of the children, to know what they do on the stage or the athletic field and to support their work in these areas. And there are times when you need to nurture self-confidence or help them navigate a rough emotional patch.

Finally, you need to be willing to work collaboratively with parents, who are an important part of life at a day school. Because you see the students so frequently and you know them in many different contexts, you feel invested in their growth and development. I loved being in the classroom every day, but I found these nonacademic responsibilities to be equally rewarding.

Q: Did you pursue your research—writing, publishing, attending conferences—outside your teaching job?

I managed to finish my book, *A Race of Singers: Whitman's Working-Class Hero From Guthrie to Springsteen* (University of North Carolina Press, 2000). It was great fun to write. I grew up in a working-class town during the height of deindustrialization and enjoyed writing about some of the artists who helped me make sense of what I was seeing and feeling at that time. I revised the manuscript before my children were born, mostly in the late-evening and early-morning hours.

I certainly don't have the time to take on another book right now, and to be honest, with two young daughters, my interest in publishing has diminished. But I try to write at least one piece a year. I've done some reviews (they range from being published in *Science*, of all places, to *Backstreets*, a Bruce Springsteen fan magazine.)

Q: How did you end up in an administrative position at Friends?

It was not a career that I had imagined, but it is one that has been extremely rewarding. Quakers have a wonderful saying: "The way opens." Those words describe my career path.

When I started teaching in a Friends school and working closely with students and families and together with colleagues, I began to recognize that teachers and administrators could work collaboratively to affect the lives of students in very profound ways. And I enjoyed the challenges of addressing practical, everyday problems. The work was so different from the research and writing that I had been doing.

I enjoyed research but ultimately found the whole process somewhat isolating. I'm very grateful that I had the opportunity to earn a PhD—I worked with wonderful people who cared deeply about what they did. But I found the relationships and the work I was doing in Quaker education, in particular, and independent schools, in general, to be much more fulfilling than the world of scholarship.

Q: How is being the head of school different from teaching?

The distinction is not as vast as you might expect, in part because I was fortunate enough to continue my career in Quaker education. There's no doubt that I have different responsibilities: fundraising, supervision of personnel, oversight of budget, to name a few. I enjoy the array of responsibilities and the fact that no two days are the same. I miss the everyday work with students in the classroom and am always looking for opportunities to connect with them. I'm hoping that I can make time to teach a class in a year or two.

Q: What qualities do you look for when hiring new teachers?

Someone once told me to hire happy people. That's some of the best advice I've ever heard. So I look for people who are excited about working with students and families. We certainly look for people who have great knowledge of their discipline, who communicate tremendous enthusiasm for learning, who encourage students to engage the world in a socially responsible and ethical manner. For us, teaching is obviously much more important than scholarship. Schools are also interested in finding teachers who can serve as coaches and advisers for such publications as the newspaper or literary magazine.

Q: What advice would you give current graduate students considering teaching at a private school?

Many graduate students bring a certain hubris when they interview for jobs at independent schools. They need to understand that our faculty members are remarkably talented, knowledgeable, and strong willed, so arrogance and a recitation on the latest theory are not likely to impress. Candidates who offer engaging and meaningful teaching demonstrations are likely to do well.

But first and foremost, a candidate needs to be able to demonstrate a genuine willingness to work with students and families and a commitment to supporting the values and mission of the school. When all is said and done, it's not likely to be a happy marriage unless the teacher embraces the mission of the school.

Looking Backward: Seven Stories

Now it's time to expand your personal inventory to include life beyond the university. Everything counts here: childhood triumphs, high school activities, half-forgotten hobbies. In this exercise, you'll look back at the whole of your life, not just your work experience, to find out what makes you happy and how you can be successful.

We've borrowed the Seven Stories approach from Kate Wendleton's *Through the Brick Wall: How to Job-Hunt in a Tight Market*—a great resource for career-changers like us. Here's how you start: Write down twenty enjoyable accomplishments from any time in your life. Include anything you enjoyed doing that you also did well. You can mix childhood memories with recent events, and big professional moments with trivial victories. Anything goes. It may take you a day or two to come up with your list of twenty. Then pick out the seven stories that speak to you most strongly: the ones that were the most satisfying, the most characteristic of who you think you are.

Next, write a paragraph about each of the seven accomplishments, describing what you did well and how it made you feel. Note the skills that you demonstrated in each circumstance. As you go through the stories, you'll notice remarkable overlap between them. The qualities that you've always taken for granted will most likely turn out to be qualities that lead to your greatest successes. We often don't give ourselves credit for certain skills because they've always just been part of who we are.

Finally, you can start to see how those skills add up to a personality profile by asking yourself a few questions on the basis of these stories: What kind of environment do I thrive in? What kind of projects do I like to work on? What skills do I enjoy using most? When am I most proud of myself?

For example, Wendleton recalls that she spent some of her happiest childhood moments orchestrating big theater productions in her neighborhood. She wrote the plays, sold the tickets, made the costumes, mixed the lemonade, and played the lead role. Combining this memory with other positive experiences in her work and personal life, she learned that she loved "running the show" as a manager and an entrepreneur.

This exercise won't help you find your perfect job tomorrow, but it will give you a framework for understanding yourself. You'll know what you're looking for long term, and you can review different careers in the meantime on the basis of whether they fit a few, some, or most of the criteria you've outlined.

SHOULD I GO TO LAW SCHOOL?

Many graduate students see law school as the next-best option when they become frustrated with academia, but it's important to think through the consequences before you take the LSAT. Instead of asking yourself "Do I want to go to law school?" you should be asking "Do I want to be a lawyer?" There's an enormous difference between the two experiences, and you should know what to expect from a law career before you spend three years and over $100K earning the degree.

Because there are many kinds of lawyers, we interviewed two different people for their perspectives on the profession: Evan Wilson left academia after six years on the job market with a PhD in English and chose the big-money, big-firm path after law school. Lola Zachary left her master's program in history without a degree and chose the lower-paying public service path.

Q: How did you research law careers before starting law school?

Wilson: Before I applied to law school, I got a job as a word processor at a big law firm in New York. It was a good way to see whether I could bear the life.

Zachary: I worked as a paralegal after grad school. It opened my eyes to a whole field of work that I don't want to do—corporate law—and pushed me toward exploring different areas of the law that I now love: prosecution and litigation.

Q: How was your experience in law school?

Wilson: The weirdest part of law school was being back in a classroom where I was not only not in charge, but I was also the stupidest, most ill-prepared person in the room. I didn't realize you could get course outlines from other students—I wasted a lot of time doing unnecessary work.

Zachary: Law school is completely different from grad school. In my master's program, at least, everything was much fuzzier. Lots of "What do you think? What do you feel? What was the author trying to say?" In law school, it's much more concrete, much more structured.

Q: What area of the law interests you the most, and why?

Wilson: I chose corporate tax almost by accident. I happened to get along with the corporate tax lawyers at my firm. They respect education; they're interested in books and opera—I could talk to them. Corporate tax is a more bookish area of law. It's more introverted.

Zachary: My favorite area of law is criminal prosecution. It's intense work, which a lot of corporate law is not. That has its benefits and drawbacks, obviously. You need to be very quick on your feet, know your law backward and forward, and be comfortable with public speaking.

Q: Do you use any of the skills you learned in graduate school in practicing law?

Wilson: Research is the skill I use most. Also, although I'm not at a level yet where my teaching skills are coming in handy, I hear that later a lot of what you do is teach complex tax codes to clients.

Zachary: I didn't use many of the skills from grad school as a paralegal. The only thing that might have applied was teaching. An ability to express myself clearly came in very handy when dealing with support staff, vendors, clients, and especially junior associates.

Q: How much debt do you have from law school, and much money did you make starting out?

Wilson: My debt from law school is between $100K and $150K. It's almost exactly equal to my first year's salary.

Zachary: I went to law school knowing that the jobs I was interested in (prosecution or smaller litigation firms) wouldn't pay the big bucks. I'm $56,000 in debt, I had help from my family for the rest; otherwise it would have easily been about $120,000. Since I'm only a law clerk this year, my salary isn't indicative of the legal market. The jobs I'm applying to for next year only make between $50K and $70K.

Q: If you did it all over again, would you still go to grad school?

Wilson: I'm glad I have a PhD because I care about readings books and understanding them, but for me, that's a private thing. I don't have a vocation for teaching. I prefer working in the legal world. I'm much happier here—it's more collegial than academe. I feel much more like people are pulling together. Academe had so many bitter fights over nothing.

Zachary: I don't really believe in changing anything. It sounds corny, but the road I took is the one I was supposed to take to get me here. If I finished my master's degree, instead of leaving without the degree, I might never have gone to law school. Working as a paralegal pushed me toward exploring areas of the law that I now love.

Guilty Pleasures

What do you when nobody's watching? How do you procrastinate? The ways in which you "waste time" can tell you a great deal about what you enjoy. For example, Sean Boocock, a doctoral student in philosophy at Notre Dame, spent his leisure hours playing video games. He originally hid this passion because it seemed like a waste of time, but eventually left his program to earn an MA in computer science and now works as a video game designer at Electronic Arts.

Another example of how this shift in perspective can lead to insight came from an engineering student who participated in a career workshop we led at Michigan State University. He had a hard time naming his interests beyond academia when we asked him directly, but when we asked, "How do you procrastinate?" he told us that he spends too much time reading investing and business news online. He said he'd always enjoyed browsing sites like MSNBC.com but felt guilty because it had nothing to do with his dissertation. To us, his confession was a breakthrough: an engineer with an interest in and understanding of finance and investing is a hot commodity. What he considered a guilty pleasure was actually a valuable asset. Instead of thinking of time spent away from your dissertation as procrastination or distraction, think of it as a window into your own preferences, skills and interests.

SHOULD I GO TO LIBRARY SCHOOL?

"Academic librarianship will be a natural fit for many PhDs in the humanities and social sciences, especially for those who are good at research," says Todd Gilman, a PhD in English and an academic librarian at Yale University.

Q: What are the best parts of being a librarian?

One of the greatest joys of library work is that I don't have to prepare lectures or grade papers but still make a meaningful contribution to college students' education.

Q: What are the challenges of being a librarian?

One of the challenges is that academic librarians are generally held in lower esteem that the teaching faculty (by both the faculty themselves and the administration).

Q: What kind of people do well in this field?

Generally speaking—and contrary to popular stereotype, I might add—those who make the best librarians are the most outgoing. You really have to be devoted to service, whether it's to serve proactively on a reference desk, to provide excellent bibliographic instruction, to do collection development creatively, or even to be a great cataloguer. Passivity and shyness will not get you very far. Enthusiasm and good people skills will.

Q: What should a PhD expect from library school?

It is difficult to generalize about library education. How good an experience you have depends mostly on the person teaching each class. The workload will seem light to medium compared with most subject-specific programs at the better graduate schools.

Q: Is library school expensive?

Most library school programs are affordable because they belong to big state schools. And if there isn't an affordable library program near you, you can take the degree online and still get in-state tuition even if you are out-of-state in some cases. Also, there are a number of grants available to PhDs who want to become librarians offered, for example, by the Association of Research Libraries (ARL) and the Institute for Museum and Library Services (IMLS) in connection with specific library school programs.

Q: What are the job prospects for librarians?

There are many would-be librarians with nothing more than a bachelor's degree and a master's in library science, and they are not in demand. But for subject specialists, like those with PhDs in English, foreign languages, history, art history, classics, economics, psychology, anthropology, and so on, the prospects are much better. Subject specialists make the best reference librarians, I believe, because of their thorough understanding of the research process. And their worth is recognized by many library search committees.

"This Is Your Brain on Graduate School"

What's going on in your head? What do you spend most of your time thinking about? Do you have interests and passions that crowd out what you're "supposed" to be doing? Are you spending too much time worrying about your adviser or your finances? Draw a map of your head, including all the clutter, and give each subject the proportional space it deserves. Be honest with yourself, but have fun.

Now redraw your head. How would you like it to look? What do you want to spend your time thinking about?

No Need for a #2 Pencil

You've exhausted all the exercises in this chapter and still don't know what to do? Try a different approach. Instead of looking at your skills, try finding a job that matches your personality. Some of us were originally drawn to academia because we love

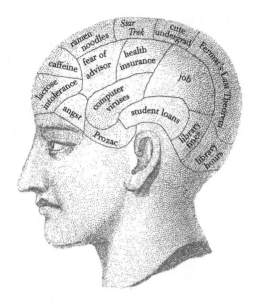

the solitary work of growing spores in petri dishes or rummaging through dusty archives. Others who thrive in a more collaborative environment may have come to graduate school to pursue a love of teaching. Getting a different perspective on your strengths and weaknesses can help you narrow down your career choices.

Self-assessment is the place to begin. Your university's career office probably offers several personality tests, but you can also find a wealth of free information on the Internet. Here are a few sites to try (because URLs change, be sure to Google for updated links):

Keirsey Temperament Sorter
http://www.keirsey.com/
Based on Carl Jung's work on "psychological types," the Keirsey Temperament Sorter asks you a series of questions and sorts you into distinct temperament types: rational, idealist, artisan, guardian. Each of the groups is then divided into four variants—one of which will match your personality. The best part of the site is seeing the famous people who match your psychological type.

Myers-Briggs Type Indicator

http://www.personalitytest.net/types/index.htm

You may have already taken this popular personality test at some point in your life. But you can take it with your workplace personality in mind, and you may find some new results. Answer sixty-eight multiple-choice questions to see where you land in the scale of the following traits: introvert/extrovert, intuition/sensation, feeling/thinking, perceiving/judging.

Job Hunter's Bible

http://www.jobhuntersbible.com/

Check out the online companion to Dick Bolles's popular career book *What Color Is Your Parachute?* to find links to a multitude of personality test sites as well as some interesting discussion of their uses and limitations.

No test is 100 percent accurate, but taking several of them can give you a better idea of your talents. Also remember that web tests tend to be more simplified than printed versions of these tests—so if you find them helpful, seek out more detailed information and resources from your university's career center.

Where Are All Those PhDs Anyway?

Now that you've taken an inventory of your skills, likes, and dislikes, it's time to start thinking about where you can put them to use. Where do PhDs work outside the academy? Everywhere. "Scratch the surface of any major company and you'll find some PhDs," assures Carol Barash, former professor and founder of Story to College, Inc., a company that teaches high school students to find their own unique stories and translate them into admissions essays.

What follows is a roundup of PhDs employed in fields from arts administration, to government, to media, to technology. Because you may not know many people working outside the academy, these descriptions are designed to help you imagine other lives.

Nonprofits, Foundations, and Institutes

Many former academics seek out nonprofit organizations as their first step outside academia. The culture of nonprofits can be particularly PhD-friendly, since many share values similar to those of universities. But beware: Don't imagine that by going to a nonprofit you're escaping from the world of money. As one PhD who worked as a nonprofit administrator cautions, "Nonprofits are just as worried about money as for-profit companies. They just have less of it."

Susan Geib, PhD in American Studies, Owner, Written Work
From her early days as a graduate student working on public history projects with museums in and around Boston, Geib knew that she liked helping nonprofit organizations tell their stories more effectively. But before she could start her own business doing just that, she knew she needed to learn more about the nuts and bolts of managing clients, budgets, and project schedules. She worked for a few years in the corporate world to gain that crucial experience before starting her own firm more than twenty years ago. She specializes in marketing communications for higher education and nonprofits. Her business is highly collaborative, she says, and involves working closely with designers, photographers, videographers, and technologists. She takes pride in the fact that her strategies and products help these institutions fulfill their missions, whether that means attracting new students, new donors or simply sharing their message with the world.

**Lily Kim, PhD in Biomedical Engineering, Associate
Director of Platform Development at the Wyss Institute for
Biologically Inspired Engineering at Harvard University**
Lily Kim worked in consulting after completing her postdoctoral fellowship but missed the sense of ownership she had over her research. She was delighted to eventually find her current position at the Wyss Institute, whose mission is "to translate high impact biomedical research out into the world." She describes her work

as "translational research." "I go to researchers and share with them what physicians actually need. They are busy with their research and don't have time to follow what clinicians are doing. I help bridge that gap." Even though she's not doing the research directly as she did as a postdoc, she feels much more connected to it than she did in consulting because she's bringing good ideas directly to market.

Richard Bennett, PhD in Comparative Literature, Senior Vice President and Managing Director, Grenzebach Glier and Associates

Richard Bennett had no intention of building a career in fundraising when he started a graduate program in comparative literature, but he has gone on to become very successful in philanthropic management. He decided not to go on the academic market after finishing his degree "because I wanted to have control over where I lived and because I wanted to be exposed to a broader array of issues and concerns in my career than I perceived success in my field to permit." He got his first job, running the Woodrow Wilson National Fellowship Foundation's "Humanities at Work" program, by networking. While there, he had the opportunity to move into a development/fundraising role at Princeton and discovered that he enjoyed it. "There is no doubt that my knowledge of the university in particular and higher education in general" helped him land the position because it helped him "to communicate with faculty members and administrators and gave me a certain level of credibility both among colleagues and with prospective donors." He also explains that "completing a PhD can require a certain entrepreneurial drive," which has helped him attain his current position as a vice president in a philanthropic consulting firm.

Arts Administration

A love of the arts has motivated countless students to pursue careers in academia. But many have discovered that there are more ways of supporting the arts than teaching them in a university.

Barbara Berrie, PhD in Chemistry, Head of Scientific Research, Conservation Division, National Gallery of Art

An avid art lover, Barbara Berrie always knew she wanted a museum career but wasn't certain how to get there. She did well in school so was encouraged to pursue a career in the sciences, culminating in a PhD in chemistry. She launched her career at the Naval Research Laboratory as a postdoctoral fellow but eventually parlayed her PhD to land a dream job in conservation science at the National Gallery. Her position allows her to combine her passions for art and scientific research by publishing articles such as "Rethinking the History of Artists' Pigments Through Chemical Analysis."

April Lynn James, PhD in Music, Mezzo-Soprano and Director of the Maria Antonia Project, Performance Artist

April Lynn James embarked on a graduate career because of her passion for baroque music and the misguided notion that "a PhD would secure me a career that paid well and would be easier to pursue than a music performance career." After completing her dissertation, she gave up on trying to obtain a faculty position because she discovered that she "disliked teaching and everything that went along with it." Today she holds a part-time job with the Social Science Research Council working with their Mellon Mays Undergraduate Fellows program and has launched her own opera company, the Maria Antonia Project.

Margit Rankin, PhD in Comparative Literature, Executive Director, Artist Trust

As Executive Director of Artist Trust, Margit Rankin leads an organization that provides financial support, career training, and professional resources for individual artists throughout the state of Washington. She has served on many community arts advisory boards over the years and was also previously the Executive Director of Seattle Arts & Letters. Her introduction to Seattle's art scene came many years ago when she relocated to Seattle from the East Coast to accept a position at the University of Washington's Simpson Center for the Humanities.

Publishing and Media

People who especially love working with language may find careers in the publishing and media fields a natural fit. Companies always need writers who can develop a message and deliver it effectively. Many alums in these fields report that having a broad and diverse audience for their writing is extremely satisfying.

Gerald Tyson, PhD in English, Publications Officer at Pew Environment Group

When he left a position as a professor at the University of Maryland, Jerry Tyson feared that he knew how to do only one thing: teach. "In fact, I had learned something much more valuable. I had learned how to learn," Tyson explains. "Subsequently, I have learned never to 'throw away' a skill. Everything you do in one job can translate to some new opportunity or challenge for another." He used his research and writing skills to transition from academia into a career in communications and now works as a Publications Officer for a division of the Pew Foundation.

Tony Russo, PhD in Psychology, CEO, Noonan Russo Communications

Tony Russo cofounded a New York public relations firm that specializes in representing pharmaceutical and biotechnology companies. He frequently hires science PhDs because he values their scientific expertise, but they have to be willing to start at the bottom, he warns. A successful job candidate at his firm must be able to write well, learn quickly, and juggle multiple clients and projects with grace.

James Levine, PhD in Education, Founder, Levine Greenberg Literary Agency

James Levine founded his own literary agency after a varied career in early childhood education and university administration. Representing authors is like coaching graduate students, but with the advantage that "I get to pick my students," as he says. Levine also fulfills his interest in research by running the Families and

Work Institute, located across the street from his agency, at the same time.

Teaching

PhDs who realize that they are born teachers probably won't be happy anywhere but in a classroom. Remember, however, that you can expand your definition of classroom beyond the boundaries of an undergraduate lecture hall. You may gain just as much satisfaction teaching high school students, corporate clients, community groups, or adult learners.

Maria Evans Eagen, PhD in Aerospace Engineering, Science Department Chair, Foxcroft School

Maria Eagan worked as an aerospace engineer for many years before starting a career as a high school teacher. She uses her "engineering experience to bring relevancy to the science and math content that I teach and to inspire and motivate students to reach for lofty goals." But she had to learn classroom management techniques and curriculum development, skills not covered in many doctoral programs.

Anna Patchias, PhD in English, Executive Director and Owner of Champion Tutoring

Anna Patchias began working for Champion Tutoring to earn extra money while she was in graduate school at the University of Virginia. Tutoring paid better than being a teaching assistant, and as she become increasingly disillusioned with academia, she devoted more time to tutoring, eventually becoming the executive director and finally purchasing the company from the founder when she decided to retire.

Tom Worden, PhD in English, Teacher and Department Chair, Upper School, Charles E. Smith Jewish Day School

After completing his PhD in English and adjuncting for a few years, Worden knew he wanted more stability and a steady income for himself and his family. He answered an ad in the *Wash-*

ington Post for an English teacher at a private school in Rockville, MD, was hired for the position, and hasn't looked back. He has found a professionally and intellectually satisfying career but advises other graduate job seekers to be patient as they search. "If in the interview you sense you are in a situation where the academic and/or social life of the school is not conducive to your growth personally and professionally," he suggests, "trust that the right situation will come along eventually."

Higher Education Administration

For those of you who don't want to stray far from campus (or are limited by a spouse's job), academic administration can offer some of the same perks as teaching. There are a growing number of full-time nonteaching and nonresearch jobs within higher education (sometimes referred to as alt-ac careers). You're still involved with the life of a university but have the opportunity to move outside the confines of your classroom. And while some university positions (in career centers or fundraising, for example) may not require a PhD, you can be confident that a university employer will appreciate the value of your advanced degree.

Rebecca Bryant, PhD in Musicology, Assistant Dean and Director of Graduate College Career Service Office, University of Illinois
Rebecca Bryant started pursuing a career in university administration even before finishing her dissertation. She likes being in a university "filled with intelligent people and . . . a diversity of fascinating ideas" but prefers working as an administrator rather than a faculty member because "it suits my planning and organizational strengths, it provides me with more variety in my work, and it suits my lifestyle choices."

Ann Kirschner, PhD in English, University Dean, Macauley Honors College, CUNY
Ann Kirschner jumped on the new media trend early. Rather than let an academic job take her far from New York after finishing her

doctorate, she answered a classified ad and started out in the world of cable television. That position put her at the forefront of Internet technology, which she parlayed into a job as founder and CEO of the National Football League's website, NFL.com. She took that experience back into the academy as head of Morningside Ventures, a for-profit Internet company created by Columbia University. Now she serves as dean of Macauley Honors College and a well-regarded advocate for digital learning.

Lisa Coleman, PhD in American Studies, Chief Diversity Office, Harvard University

Lisa M. Coleman is the chief diversity officer for Harvard University where she is responsible for developing a strategic approach for promoting diversity across campus. She began her career teaching American studies and women's studies at the college level and later consulted with organizations such as the Association of American Medical Colleges and Merrill Lynch.

Tara Christie Kinsey, PhD in English, Princeton University, Associate Dean, Office of the Vice President for Campus Life, Office of the Dean of the College, Princeton University

Tara Christie Kinsey found a way to combine several passions: her fascination with contemporary British and Irish literature, her passion for collegiate athletics, and her love of campus life. She works at the intersection of the Office of the Dean of the College and the Office for the Vice President for Campus Life. As a dean she works primarily with student athletes, a position she knows well since she herself was a varsity softball player while an undergraduate at Princeton. She also serves as a lecturer in the English department where she continues to research and write on contemporary Irish poetry.

Anna Marie Trester, PhD in Linguistics, Director, MA Program in Language and Communication, Georgetown University

When Trester transitioned from being a student at Georgetown to an administrator, she saw the university, and her own capabilities, in a new light. She has succeeded by combining skills she had cultivated before graduate school (counseling and event-planning skills from her experience as a college resident adviser, skills in managing budgets and finance acquired at a past job as an analyst at Goldman Sachs) with expertise acquired in her doctoral program. "One of the most surprising things that I realized is that graduate training in linguistics made me very good at asking for things (and getting what I wanted), particularly in e-mails. I realized that I had been trained (almost without realizing how practical and applicable it was) in sensitivity to the nuances of audience design and positioning, which gave me an advantage in writing unignorable e-mails!"

Government and Research

Academics have found satisfying work in almost all offices of federal and state government, from the Smithsonian Institution to the National Park Service. Many of those we interviewed encourage candidates to persevere, since government hiring requires several months, many forms, and lots of patience to complete.

Sylvia Chou, PhD in Linguistics, Master's in Public Health, Program Director, Health Communication and Informatics Research Branch, National Cancer Institute, National Institutes of Health (NIH)

Sylvia Chou's training in sociolinguistics didn't make her an obvious fit for a career with the NIH. But a supervisor introduced her to a contact at the Institute and she found out about careers in scientific communications that she hadn't previously known existed. Combining her PhD with a Master's in Public Health (MPH) made her ideally suited for position in which she leads a number of multidisciplinary research projects on the role of new technologies and social media in health and health care.

"Have a sense of humility and self-awareness," she advises graduate job hunters. "I think too often the academic culture encourages us to think what we are doing is so important (and even more important than others' work) and we forget how limited our knowledge/skills are in the grand scheme of things."

Julia Huston Nguyen, PhD in History, Senior Program Officer at the National Endowment for the Humanities (NEH)

Julia Huston Nguyen left a tenure-track position at a large university because while she loved historical research and writing, she found that teaching was not an activity she could see herself doing for several years. While "teaching introductory U.S. history to 100 or 150 undergraduates, many of whom resented the state's requirement that they take the course," she came across "a job ad from the NEH, sent in an application, and (several long months later) received an offer."

"I love my job," she explains, "I work in an office full of humanities PhDs, so I have found that vibrant intellectual environment outside the academy. I love being a generalist again. I get to read proposals from every discipline in the humanities, which is a window to some of the newest and best work that's being done. I also like feeling that my work is really helping people. I help applicants get funded, and those grants do a great deal of good for teachers and college/university faculty."

Colleen Shogan, PhD in Political Science, Deputy Director, Congressional Research Service (CRS)

Colleen Shogan was a tenure-track assistant professor when she won an American Political Science Association Congressional Fellowship to support a year of work on Capitol Hill. At the end of the year she received a job offer in the Senate and decided to leave the tenure track. She transitioned into a position with the Congressional Research Service and worked her way up to Deputy Director in a few years. Her graduate training prepared her well to do policy analysis research at CRS, but she needed to develop skills not learned in her doctoral program to advance her career. "Facilitating disputes, finding compromises, and motivating others are skills that are not typically learned in graduate school. You need to pick them up as you progress in your career, or find a mentor who can help you work to acquire them," she advises.

Sharyl Nass, PhD in Cell and Tumor Biology, Director, National Cancer Policy Forum at the Institute of Medicine

While doing a postdoctoral fellowship, Sharyl Nass was active in the Johns Hopkins Postdoctoral Association, where she drafted a policy proposal for postdoctoral training. The combination of this experience and some savvy networking led her to a science policy position at the Institute of Medicine, which advises the president on health policy. Frustrated by the "grueling academic career track," she now directs a forum about cancer prevention and treatment. Being a policy analyst allows her to "function as a lifelong graduate student but earn a living wage with good benefits."

Technology Companies

Many PhDs have found challenging work in the technology sector. And it's not just math and computer science grads who thrive in tech careers; humanities and social science scholars are also skilled at learning the language of technology.

Adarsh Pandit, PhD in Biochemistry/Biophysics, Web Developer, Thoughtbot.com

"It began to dawn on me about two thirds of the way through my doctoral program that I didn't really want to go through the process of applying for postdocs," Pandit explains. "That just really wasn't appealing for me." With the support of his adviser, he researched other career paths and ended up with a job at McKinsey Consulting after finishing his doctorate at the University of Chicago. "Networking is key," he explains, not only for the job search but for professional development throughout your career. "The one thing I have realized is the most useful tool for every career is really becoming adept at networking in an honest way— meeting people and saying 'Hey, I'm really interested in what you're doing.'"

After a few years in consulting he became interested in development, so he taught himself key technical skills with online tutorials, by collaborating with others, and by reading a lot of books. (One great thing about changing careers is that once you do it, it's not so frightening to do it again). He developed enough expertise to land several contract jobs and now works with thoughtbot, a Boston-based consultancy that builds web and mobile applications.

Geoff Davis, PhD Applied Mathematics, Staff Quantitative User Experience Researcher, Google

Geoff Davis took a leave of absence from his post as an assistant professor at Dartmouth for a one-year assignment at Microsoft. "After a great deal of soul-searching," he decided to quit his academic job. "I decided that I was more interested in having people use the results of my research than in writing lots of papers." He began working on researching ways to improve Microsoft's digital audio player. "To put things in perspective, maybe a hundred or so people read my academic papers. The last Windows Media Audio player, on the other hand, was downloaded by two million people on the day it came out and was recently estimated to have forty million users." He continued to expand his reach when he moved to Google and used his data science expertise to build Google AdWords.

Create Your Own Possibilities

These alumni profiles are just a small sample of the possibilities that are open to you. We hope we've helped jump-start your imagination. Now it's up to you to find out more about the fields that interest you. In the next chapter, you'll learn how to expand the options we've listed above by conducting information interviews with alumni and doing informal internships. As you learn more about how other people have organized their careers around their skills and interests, you'll develop a stronger sense of what's right for you.

....

POST-ACADEMIC PROFILE:
SAMANTHA SUTTON, PHD IN BIOLOGY, LIFE COACH

Few of us will have a classic Eureka moment—bathtub and all—that provides the answer to years of career exploration, but Samantha Sutton did.

As a graduate student in synthetic biology at the Massachusetts Institute of Technology, she initially had a difficult time picturing herself as anything other than a scientist or engineer. Her desire to work as part of a team had already led her to consider nonacademic work, such as joining a biotech start-up. But one moment of epiphany radically changed her direction.

Oddly enough, the answer had been in front of her all along. Sutton had taken a "life coaching" course at MIT, which was designed to help students and staff find their passions and actively design their lives. It was while working as a teaching assistant for that course that she realized that coaching itself was her passion.

"I took the course, served as a teaching assistant, and helped develop a curriculum so it could be taught at other institutions. About a year in, I started to think to myself, "Wow, these coaches have the best jobs ever. To be let in to someone's life like that, and then help them take on the big issues—that must be an amazing career," she recalls. "But I didn't really think it was an option for me. I was Scientist Samantha, and scientists don't become life coaches."

"Then one day, I was sitting in a bathtub at a scientific conference in Austria, and I realized that personal development had actually been a consistent theme running throughout my life. Before graduate school, I taught English in rural Thailand, and had spent seven weeks meditating at a Buddhist monastery. At MIT, I had become a certified mediator. I had considered each of those passions to be random blips, but in that bathtub in Austria, I realized that they formed a pattern. I enjoy thinking about my own personal evolution and helping that evolution in others. Maybe, I thought, Scientist Samantha could become Coach Samantha. So I approached the coaches at the Handel Group (the group that taught life coaching at MIT) and told them of my realization, and they said 'Of course. What took you so long?' I trained with the company while finishing up my PhD, and after graduation started working there as a coach."

She advises current graduate students, "If you think you don't know what makes you happy, you probably do know but just aren't listening to yourself. Get out of your daily life and try out different activities, roles, and situations, and look for clues."

3 Asking The Big Questions

How to Figure Out If You Want Them and If They Want You

Whenever we give talks on university campuses, we inevitably hear the following complaint from at least one frustrated graduate student: "I've sent out hundreds of résumés, but I haven't gotten a single interview. What am I doing wrong?" Does this scenario sound familiar to you? Do you feel like you're working hard on your job search but getting zero results? Maybe you're starting to wonder if anyone is ever going to hire you.

Never fear. The problem isn't you—it's your job hunting strategy. If you've been measuring your efforts in terms of quantity (how many résumés have I sent out?) instead of quality (how much new information have I learned?), then it's time to shift your focus. In this chapter we'll explain why sending out lots of résumés can actually *reduce* your chances of getting an interview and then show you step-by-step how to change your approach for better results.

The first step in adopting a "quality over quantity" job hunting approach is getting specific about the kind of work you want to do. In chapter 2, we encouraged you to free yourself from the "I am my dissertation" box and think big. We urged you to imagine yourself in careers that might never have occurred to you before. Now it's time to make those dreams a reality and find a real-world job that matches up with your interests, priorities, skills, and passions. And it's at just this point in the job search where most of us go astray.

Most people engaged in a job search (and we're not just talking about academics here—this is universal human behavior) spend the bulk of their time surfing for job postings online and sending out résumés in response to ads. Some will send out résumés blindly to a company or organization they admire, hoping that the human resources department at, say, Google, will match them up with whatever job would suit them best. Or they figure that if a job is advertised online, they might as well apply since the position is vacant—can't hurt, right? There's always time to learn more about the job later if you're invited for an interview. Why waste time up front? Just send out lots of résumés and see who responds.

But here's the problem: If *you* aren't willing to invest the time to figure whether you are right for a particular job, why would someone else care enough to do it for you? You're the one who needs a job, so it's your responsibility. Human resources professionals are seeking people who fit specific profiles, and if your materials do not make a persuasive case for why you are a great match for a particular position, you are unlikely to get anything more than a cursory glance. If you have ever thought to yourself, "I did well today, I sent out thirty résumés," we're sorry to tell you that your time has not been well spent. Of course, you may have sensed this yourself and been discouraged by the lack of response. Christine Kelly, a Graduate Student Career Consultant at University of California–Irvine, sees this phenomenon every day. "Now that everything is online, people think that sitting at a computer means they are job searching," Kelly says. She cautions graduate students that "papering the planet" doesn't work. "Just because you sent an e-mail, that doesn't mean anyone read it. You need to make human contact."

We couldn't agree more. The truth is that the more research you do up front, the better your chances of being invited to an interview. It's up to you to figure out where you might fit best in an organization and to build an argument for yourself in terms that are meaningful and relevant to the employer.

The idea that you should research a job before you apply will sound strange to anyone coming from academia. When you apply for a faculty position, you already know the job requirements, the workplace environment, the kind of person who's likely to be a good match, etc. And hiring committees are already quite familiar with PhDs like yourself. So during a faculty search, the focus is primarily on the essence of your scholarly nature: What kind of teacher are you? How innovative is your research? Will you do great things over the next few decades?

Outside of academia, the tables are turned: what matters most is how well you match the organization's needs and how much you can contribute to helping them reach their goals. It's not about you, it's about them. This is an enormous shift in perspective, and the more fully you understand and embrace it, the more successful you will be, not only in your post-academic job search, but throughout your post-academic career. Most of the major missteps that graduate students or former academics make in their job searches beyond academia—such as having a too-long, too-detailed résumé, or talking endlessly about their dissertation topic in a job interview—can be attributed to a failure to grasp this crucial difference.

So here is our advice: Before you apply for a job, learn what that employer wants. You should do *more* research than you think necessary, and do it much *earlier* in the process than you planned. Find out everything you can about the job and the organization and then demonstrate that specific knowledge in your résumé and cover letter. Why invest all this time up front? Because submitting a customized and well-researched cover letter and résumé—to a job for which you are actually qualified—is a critical first step toward getting an interview. Sue reviews hundreds of résumés every week as an executive search consultant and she can assure you that this approach will indeed make you stand out. So few people take the time to research openings and tailor their résumé and cover letters accordingly that doing so will give you an immediate advantage over the rest of the pack.

There's another important benefit to doing your research before you apply. It gives you a chance to figure out if this is truly the right job for you. Would you be happy in it? Would it offer you the kind of challenges and opportunities that you're looking for? If not, then you shouldn't apply. You've probably heard that a job interview is a two-way street, that you are interviewing the organization as much as they are interviewing you. It's the same principle. Be stingy with your résumé. Take the time to learn what's out there, and make sure you only apply to jobs that are a good, strong match for you. You are a valuable commodity, and we don't want you to waste your time pursuing an opportunity that you wouldn't want or enjoy.

And finally, as you're doing this research, you'll discover that you are naturally and painlessly networking, which is the best way to get a job. We're sure you've heard by now that networking is the number one way to get a job, but it probably still sounds like an awkward, alien process. Read on to learn more about our step-by-step strategies for simple and effective networking, as an integrated part of your job research process.

Asking the Big Questions

So, what exactly do we mean by doing your research up front? What kind of research? And how are you supposed to go about it? In this section, first we'll explain the kind of information you should be seeking, and then we'll outline several different strategies for obtaining it. Let's start with the Big Questions. A good way to measure whether your job search is emphasizing quality or quantity

---

THE BIG QUESTIONS

About the Organization
- In your own words, what does this organization do? Who are its key clients, donors, partners, audience, etc? What makes it tick?
- How does this organization get the resources to do its work? What are its primary revenue streams? If it's a non-profit, what are its main funding sources?
- What other organizations do similar work to this one? Who are its peers? Its competitors? How do they differ from each other?

- What threats lie ahead for this organization? What opportunities does it have to grow?

About the Industry
- What are the key trends that someone working in this industry would be following? Are there forces that might change its work or mission over the next decade?
- What publications/websites would I be reading or associations would I belong to if I worked in this field?
- What's the employment outlook—are companies hiring now in this industry? What are the larger factors that might cause there to be more/fewer job openings in this industry in the future?
- Is this kind of work limited to certain geographical areas? Which ones?
- What other jobs/organizations similar to this one might I be interested in?

About the Position
- In your own words, what would you do all day in this job?
- Who would you be your colleagues? To whom would you report? Who would report to you? What are the backgrounds, skills, personality types of these people likely to be?
- What are the skills and qualities that someone needs to do this job well?
- What is the path upward from this position? Where might someone go next, either within this organization or elsewhere?
- How do people changing careers generally get started in this field? At what level? What skills/education/ abilities do most people hired at that level bring?
- What's the quality of life for someone in this line of work? Is there travel required? Long hours?

About Yourself
- Why would this particular job be a good match for my particular skills, abilities, values, and temperament?
- Am I a viable prospect for this job right now? Or do I need additional skills or experience first? If so, what kind?

is to ask yourself how many of the Big Questions you can answer about the job you're currently most interested in pursuing.

How did you do? If you could answer half of the Big Questions about a job that interests you, then you're on the right track. The Big Questions are the starting point for your research, so you don't need to have all the answers before you apply for a job, but you should be well on your way. And if you keep the Big Questions close at hand, you'll find that they will guide you through every phase of the job search. the Big Questions will not only help you write a persuasive and powerful résumé and cover letter; they will also help you prepare for an interview, negotiate salary and benefits, and even evaluate whether or not you are on the right career path over the long term. In this chapter, we'll focus on the value of the Big Questions in deciding which organizations are worthy to receive your résumé, but we'll refer back to them again in later chapters as well.

Answering the Big Questions: Three Strategies

As a graduate student, you have a natural advantage when it comes to research. No one is better prepared than you are to track down the best resources, collect data, formulate hypotheses, analyze results, and construct theories. To answer the Big Questions, you'll draw upon all these skills. You may find the terrain a little unfamiliar, however, if you have never worked outside academia, so in this section we'll offer specific approaches and step-by-step suggestions to help you get started.

We recommend three different strategies for seeking the answers to the Big Questions:

- Research via online resources
- Research via people
- Research via hands-on experience.

You can work through the approaches in the order listed, try all three at once, or mix and match. No matter how you go about it, we encourage you to collect as much as information as you can, from as many perspectives as possible. There is no single answer to any of the Big Questions, and that's the whole point. Pursuing the Big Questions is an ongoing process—it's what your job search is all about. You won't be finished with the Big Questions in a week or in a month or even in a year. There's always more to learn. And that's how it should be. As your career progresses, you should be continually revisiting these questions and refining your answers as you learn and grow in each new situation. But for now, let's focus on how to get enough information to write a powerful, tailored résumé and cover letter, which is the topic of chapter 4.

Research via Online Resources

The amount of publicly available information on any given organization is astounding, and yet shockingly few job seekers bother to do some basic Googling about a company before submitting a résumé. (Or if they do, they don't show evidence of it in their résumés and cover letters.) Roll up your sleeves and dive into these online resources to begin answering the Big Questions for yourself:

- Company/organization's website: Read staff member bios, the history of the organization, recent press releases etc. What are the major topics/functions of the website? Who is its audience? Look for clues about the group's priorities, culture, and future plans.
- The websites of peers and competitor organizations: How is the organization you're interested in different from/similar to its peer and competitors? Can you find the names of still other peers/competitors to research?
- Major newspapers (*New York Times*, *Washington Post*, etc.): Use the company's name as a search term to see how it turns up in the news. Does it have a global presence as well as a domestic one? If so, where?
- LinkedIn: Browse profiles of people who work at the organiza-

tion. What are the most common job titles? Which ones seem like they might be a match for you? How do your skills and experience match up? Sign up to "follow" the organization on LinkedIn.

- Other social media: Does the company have a Twitter presence? Does it have a monthly e-mail newsletter? Sign up for any and all updates to expand your knowledge base.

- Industry-specific website, blogs, etc.: Is there an association to which your target organization might belong? If it were a person, what would it be reading online?

- GuideStar: GuideStar.org gives access to financial and tax records of nonprofit organizations (the most common is a 1099 form). You can get a limited amount of information for free, more if you pay for membership. Ask your career center if they have a membership or can help you locate more tax-filing-related info on the organizations that interest you.

- EDGAR: (http://www.sec.gov/edgar.shtml): All companies doing business in the U.S. are required to file registration statements, periodic reports, and other forms electronically with the Securities and Exchange Commission through EDGAR. Anyone can access and download this information for free.

- Your university librarian: It may be so obvious that you didn't even think of it—ask a librarian to help you answer the Big Questions. Are there publications or databases specific to the industry that you might not know about?

- Your university's career center: One-stop shopping for both online resources and a database full of helpful alumni. Don't skip this step—the career center will have lots of online resources in addition to helpful career advisors. You have no idea what you don't know, right?

This list is intended only as a starting point—you'll discover many other resources along the way. And as you already know from your own academic research, the more you learn, the more you'll discover how much there is to know. "I call it 'the footnote trail,'" says Katja Zelljadt, associate director of the Stanford Hu-

MAKING THE MOST OF LINKEDIN

While you're probably familiar with the basic functions of LinkedIn, you may not realize exactly how powerful a tool it can be. The secret to unlocking all that LinkedIn has to offer is upgrading the level of your membership so you can access the advanced search features. (It's not cheap to upgrade, but you can buy one month of premium membership, search your heart out, then step back down to the basic level.) What's so great about advanced search on LinkedIn? It allows you to search by criteria that are highly relevant to your career exploration. So, you could search LinkedIn for people who have PhDs, live in your city, and work in management consulting. Or, you could look for people who work in the pharmaceutical industry and speak Mandarin. And you can even search within particular organizations, for example, to see if there is someone working at Google or the National Science Foundation, either now or in the past, who might be a good contact for you. And when you locate someone who seems like he or she could help you answer some of the Big Questions, you can contact them directly via LinkedIn, even if their e-mail address is not publicly available.

One caveat: Make sure your own LinkedIn page is ready for prime time before you start researching potential contacts on LinkedIn. The first thing people will do when you contact them is check out your own profile, so take the time to make sure your page looks at least as polished as your résumé.

manities Center and a PhD in German history. "You start at one place, you look at one footnote, and that leads you to another, and to another, and you eventually discover the new source you've never heard of before." It's the same when you research organizations online, she says, "You look at one foundation and that leads you to another organization or to another person and you keep following the trail as it keeps unfolding." Do your own trailblazing online and see how many of the Big Questions you can answer.

THE WISDOM OF STARTING AT THE BOTTOM

When Tony Russo got his first job on Wall Street, he thought that having his PhD in psychology should count in his favor, that he should make a little extra money. "They quickly disabused me of that notion, and it was a hard pill to swallow," he remembers. "I told them I'd spent eight years in grad school, and they said they were glad to have me, but the degree didn't count" as relevant experience.

Russo now sits on the other side of the hiring desk and finds that he shares the view of his former employers. As he interviews PhDs for jobs at the biotech/health care public relations firm he cofounded, Russo cautions job applicants that "if they want to switch careers, they will have to pay their dues." He looks for people who are not arrogant about their abilities. No matter how impressive their academic credentials, new hires must be willing to learn public relations from the ground up, and that often means starting with a lower salary than they expect.

However, there's an advantage to starting out at the bottom, Russo explains. "If you only have the skills for a $35K per year job, you shouldn't be in a $55K per year job. The employer will have unrealistic expectations for you, you'll miss out on learning fundamental skills, and others in the company will resent your leapfrogging over them." But if you start low, you can move up quickly and have a string of successes, Russo explains. "We've promoted people within six weeks," he adds.

Research via People

You didn't think you could get through a career guide without hearing about networking, did you? And you are probably dreading what comes next. After all, you've heard over and over again that networking is the number one way that people find jobs, but it probably sounds awkward and superficial and just plain weird to you. We get it. That's one reason that we're calling networking "research via people" instead: to reinforce that what you're really doing is seeking answers to the Big Questions through conversations with other humans. Information interviewing is another synonym for networking, but that term has a formal undertone that feels a bit dated, so we're going to focus on a more flexible and more digitally driven concept of networking instead.

Jennifer Stone Gonzalez, a PhD in communications who took an internship at a telecommunications company in order to jumpstart her career, describes the nature of networking beautifully:

> In the business world, the most important information flows through people, not texts. Most of what you learn in business comes from informal dialogue, whether in person, on the phone, or via e-mail.

A big change from academia, no? Being aware of this cultural difference is a key first step in becoming a skilled networker. And speaking of steps, you can tackle this challenge one level at a time. Start out with easier networking conversations—such as calling an alum from your own program—and work your way up to more complex interactions as you gain confidence and experience. And we promise you—networking is easier than you think. As Adarsh Pandit, a PhD in biochemistry and biophysics from the University of Chicago, said of his early career exploration conversations: "I was really surprised that people were so obliging and that there was so much goodwill to just get on the phone with some nobody and answer questions for thirty minutes. That really struck me as surprising, but over time you realize that's the oil that makes the machine go."

One key point to keep in mind as you're networking, however, is that you never want to make anyone feel that you are asking them for a job. Instead, let the people you contact know that you're primarily looking for their perspectives and advice at the moment, rather than a job. Yes, of course you're job hunting, and they will understand that's the real reason that you are doing this research. But this fig leaf is a critical feature of any successful networking interaction because it frees the other person from the fear that they will be asked to help someone they've just met find a job at their own firm. Of course, if they think you are a good match they may well offer you additional help, but you want to leave that option entirely to their discretion.

Our goal in this section is to make networking (aka researching the Big Questions through people) not only bearable for you, but productive and even enjoyable. Below we offer two simple, concrete strategies that take the guesswork out of networking. Whether you start with the lower-risk approaches or jump in at the deep end, bear in mind that your objective is seeking answers to the Big Questions.

Technique 1: Talk to Other Graduate Alumni

Researching what graduate alumni from your own department are doing now is a great way to start your own career exploration, especially if you have no idea what you want might want to do next. And if you're nervous about networking, you'll find that other graduate alumni–whether you share an alma mater or not—are generally more approachable and empathetic because they have been where you are now.

So how do you get started? Here are some basic steps:

• **Who:** Start with graduate alumni from your own department. This is your natural audience. You can then expand your reach to graduate alumni from other departments or other universities. Because your goal is to talk in general about life outside academia, you don't need to worry too much about whether their current career is an exact fit for you. These are "big picture" conversations as well as a great opportunity to practice applying the Big Questions.
• **How:** Most universities have an online alumni database. Search for people who went through your program but now work in other fields. Select three people you'd like to talk to as a starting point. If you're having trouble finding relevant alumni to contact, make an appointment with career services to ask for advice about navigating the database more effectively.

- **Goal:** Think of these conversations as getting advice from someone who's already been down the road you're on and can point out the potholes and pancake houses. Ask about the person's experience in graduate school, their job search (both academic and post-academic), and their current career path. How did they make the transition? What did they learn in doing so?

- **P.S.:** Don't forget to send a thank-you e-mail after the conversation. And file away the names of the people you talked to—you never know when you might want to reach out to them again, possibly even years from now.

Technique 2: Send a Two-Question E-mail

The Two-Question E-mail is another great way to build your confidence around networking but, unlike the graduate alumni conversations described above, this technique focuses more directly on seeking answers to the Big Questions about your field of interest. Your best target for this approach is someone who has a connection to a field or career that you'd like to explore. It's great if they hold an advanced degree, attended your alma mater, have a friend in common with you, live in your city, etc., so you have a natural point of connection, but it isn't necessary. The primary focus here is gaining more specific information about a particular field.

- **Who:** You might find these people among your institution's graduate alumni, but you will most likely turn them up from your online research. Scour the websites of organizations that interest you (and don't forget about LinkedIn) for bios of likely contacts and select a few to approach.

- **How:** E-mail the person directly with a very brief note. Do not go into detail about your dissertation or your job search. This e-mail is not about you, it's about them. State your common interest or connection briefly, if you have one, and say that you are a graduate student in X who is interested in learning more about careers in their field. Adding a brief sentence explain-

...ng why their field appeals to you is fine, but keep it short. (Note to those who tend toward excessive candor: "Because the academic job market is terrible" is not a reason why their field appeals to you.) Ask the person if they would be willing to answer two questions via e-mail about breaking into the field. This phrasing is important. Limiting it to two questions assures them that you won't take much time. Answering via e-mail assures them it will be more convenient than having to schedule a call. And saying you want to "break into" a field assures them you are asking for career transition advice, rather than a job. You'll find that most people will be glad to help. And then you're set: ask them two of the Big Questions.

- **Goal:** Your goal is to get comfortable with networking via a structured, low-risk interaction and to add a name to your list of networking contacts. As you gain confidence, you'll be able to deploy this tool consistently and strategically to help tackle your Big Questions.
- **P.S.** After they answer, thank them warmly for their help and promise them that you will follow up on their advice. Finally, ask if you may touch base again down the line if you have more questions in the future.

If you try the techniques above, you'll discover that some people will have wonderfully nuanced and helpful answers for you, and others will be a dead end. That's just how it works. Networking is not linear and your results will be unpredictable and uneven. The key to success in networking is continuing to reach out, make connections and gather answers to the Big Questions, because networking absolutely works if you are willing to invest the time. And as you get more comfortable with networking and as your job search progresses, you can go back to these contacts and ask them for different kinds of help, such as suggesting other people in the field you might contact, or asking them for a "real world" review of your résumé. These techniques are your training wheels, and whenever you're ready, you can take them off and zip away on your own.

Research via Hands-On Experience

In chapter 1 we talked about the value of keeping one foot outside of academia in the form of a part-time job, hobby, volunteer work, etc. and how such experiences can even unexpectedly lead to a new career. Our emphasis in that chapter was on maintaining a healthy emotional and psychological balance and keeping your graduate work and career prospects in perspective. In this chapter, we're going to talk about part-time jobs and volunteer work again but from a different vantage point. We're going to focus on a more intentional and targeted approach to hands-on experience—the kind that is designed from the start to help you learn more about the Big Questions and further prepare you for a new career.

You may be thinking, "I have rent to pay—I can't afford to do an internship. I need a full-time job, now." We understand that pressure. But too often job changers bring an "all or nothing" mentality to their search and try to move directly into a full-time, highly competitive position instead of starting with a more readily achievable intermediate step. We would argue that doing an internship or volunteer stint is actually a faster route to full-time employment when you have no relevant experience. Give yourself an easier win and set yourself up for future success by adding some kind of hands-on experience to your list of ways to answer the Big Questions. A little bit of exposure to a new field will not only give you the chance to see whether it truly is something you want to do but will also expand your network, inform your résumé and cover letter, and make you a generally more desirable candidate for a full-time job.

Here's a great example of what we mean: chemistry PhD Robert Rich planned his exit from academia by volunteering in the field he wanted to enter. While doing a postdoc at the National Institutes of Health, he arranged with his adviser to spend one day a week volunteering in the Office of Science and Policy Programs at the American Association for the Advancement of Science. "This arrangement enabled me to pay my rent and also get my foot in the door." When a job opened at AAAS a few months later, "I was the natural choice," Rich says.

Your university's career center is another great way to find internships, whether formal or informal, at places that interest you. And how about volunteer work? That's always a good way to get your foot in the door. Temp work can also provide a crash course in another field. Try asking several different temp agencies to place you at a certain company or in an industry that interests you. They know that offering a client a smart cookie like yourself is a real coup and will often go out of their way to accommodate you. And if you're temping in the right kind of company, people will realize quickly that you have a lot more to offer than your coffee-making skills. You can learn the business and make some contacts, not a bad deal for a month-long investment. (In fact, temping is exactly how Sue got one of her early breaks.)

Finally, you can always create your own hands-on experience. Your experience doesn't have to be formal or officially sanctioned. Does the job you're interested in require knowing how to read a basic balance sheet, but you can't find any internships that will teach you that skill? Then teach yourself. Google "how to read a balance sheet" and you'll find YouTube videos and other resources at your fingertips for free. Free and low-cost online classes are available everywhere with more being added every day in every subject you can imagine. You have no excuse for being uninformed about anything that might interest you. Continue your research into the Big Questions and prepare yourself for a new field by diving into the thousands of videos, tutorials, articles, and other online resources available to you.

You can take this spirit of self-direction off-line as well, and apply it to the world around you. Maybe you're interested in fundraising and have taken Philanthropy 101 online but now want to see how it feels to work in the field. If a volunteer or internship program doesn't exist near you, then create your own opportunity by approaching any nonprofit you care about (the library, the animal shelter, etc.) and ask if you can help with fundraising. If you're open to helping with whatever tasks they need done, you have a good chance of hearing a "yes" to your request.

Transitional Tales

Katja Zelljadt, Associate Director, Stanford Humanities Center

Katja had always wanted to work in a museum but quickly discovered that having a PhD in German history rather than American history hampered her job search. So, while in graduate school at Harvard, she worked part-time in one of the university's museums as a way of getting some on-the-ground experience. Her job was a low-level administrative one and included such tasks as photocopying travel receipts and submitting expense reports for reimbursement.

In the course of doing these routine tasks, however, Katja began reading the receipts she was processing and became curious about the work of a consultant that the museum had recently hired. She asked her supervisor about the consulting project, and he told her that the consultant was talking with faculty, administrators, and museum staff about how best to integrate the museum's collections into the curriculum. When Katja asked, "And what about the student perspective?" he realized that she had identified an important oversight.

Katja volunteered to poll the students in her classes about how they use the museum's holdings in their work and shared her findings with her supervisor. Fascinated by the curricular question at hand, Katja then asked, "Would you find it helpful if I researched it more?" With her supervisor's blessing, she set up phone interviews with curators around the country and prepared a report on best practices for integrating art collections with curricula.

Of course, none of this work fell within the scope of her minimum-wage job, but she learned about a side of the museum that she never knew existed before and built relationships with museum curators around the country. And when she applied

WHAT DOES IT TAKE TO GET A JOB IN CONSULTING?

"For many graduate students, consulting seems like an ideal career option. But I think that has more to do with ego and less to do with truly understanding what consulting is about," says David Attis, a former management consultant for A.T. Kearney who now serves as a Practice Manager for the Education Advisory Board. Anne Coyle, who formerly led McKinsey's recruiting of individuals with advanced degrees (other than MBAs), concurs that the reality of consulting is quite different from what you might imagine: "It's not as sexy and cerebral as you think. As a new hire, you'll be doing mostly process-oriented work that is not terribly interesting. And you have to be willing to spend Monday–Thursday away from home, every week, on a client site, with Friday spent at your home office."

Before you send out a single résumé, invest the time to figure out for yourself what a life in consulting might look like and whether it's right for you. How? By striving to answer the Big Questions in this chapter. Once you've done your research into various consulting firms (remembering they are all different), then you can take full advantage of Attis and Coyle's advice for breaking into consulting:

- **Academic success alone is not enough**: Attis and Coyle agree that top-notch academic credentials are a given, not a differentiator. Every candidate they see has excelled academically, so you'll need more than that to stand out. For McKinsey in particular, Coyle says, the baseline is incredibly high. Unless you have near-perfect GRE scores and have graduated at the top of your class from the nation's most elite universities, you are unlikely to advance in their recruiting process.

- **Build your skills**: Attis is always looking for transferrable skills and signs that a person will adjust well to a corporate environment. He recommends volunteer work or a gig in your own university's administration. "If you've worked in an office, on a deadline, producing something that isn't an academic publication—that's something I would like to see." Or use a summer for something other than your dissertation, he advises. "That would lower the risk for me in hiring you."

- **Practice for the case interview:** You can expect a consulting firm interview to involve solving "cases," hypothetical business problems that you work through with your interviewer. The case is designed to test your analytical and problem-solving skills, rather than your knowledge. At McKinsey, the case interview is all-important, says Coyle. But Coyle and Attis agree that case interviewing is a skill anyone can learn with time and practice. There are plenty of resources available online and in your university's career center, so make sure you are ready to ace the case if you get the call.

- **Speak positively about your career change:** "If someone is feeling like a failure because they haven't landed an academic job, that usually comes through very clearly in an interview. You need to put a positive spin on it. I don't want to feel like a consolation prize," Attis says. He suggests finding ways to reframe your thinking, such as, "I found my interests gradually changing" or "I found that what I liked most about being in academia was figuring out what made things tick and coming up with ways to improve them."

- **Be flexible about your home base:** You can improve your chances of being hired if you don't restrict yourself geographically, Coyle says. Everyone wants to work from the San Francisco or New York office, but if you're willing to be based wherever you might be needed, you have a better shot.

- **Don't overlook smaller firm opportunities:** While everyone knows the name McKinsey, the fact is that they hire 1–2 percent of applicants each year. You can expand your options by identifying smaller consulting firms that might actually be a better match for you and may be willing to take the risk on someone without much experience beyond academia, says Attis. Some firms specialize in an industry (pharmaceuticals, for example, which might be a great match for a chemist) and others do general management consulting but without the enormous global infrastructure.

As you can see, the world of consulting has its own distinct culture, so the more you learn about its conventions in advance, the stronger you'll appear as a potential candidate.

to work at the Getty Research Institute the following year, her supervisor gave her a glowing reference, praising her initiative and resourcefulness. Although she has since moved on to Stanford from the Getty position, she continues to advocate for the importance of bringing curiosity and imagination to even the most menial of tasks. "You are always learning," Katja says, "so none of your time is wasted."

William Van Trump, Senior Engineer, Illumina

William Van Trump, a PhD in biological sciences from University of California–Irvine, proves that scientists too can change their stripes. Van Trump was an expert in how fish detect flow—"not the most marketable specialty," he acknowledges—and found that the turning point in his year-long job search was taking a temporary position at Intel in an electrochemistry lab. He knew nothing about electrochemistry, but he read up and learned the field. The experience enabled him not only to put the name Intel at the top of his résumé but also provided potential employers with solid evidence of his ability to excel in areas of science unrelated to his dissertation.

When William was offered the temporary position at Intel, he was many months into his job search and had been sending out dozens of résumés each week, with few results. So, he felt he had little to lose and spent six months at Intel in the temporary position, earning more than he had as a graduate student but less than he would have as a postdoc. Intel had a strict policy of never converting temporary employees to permanent ones, so he knew there was no future for him at Intel when the position ended. He therefore continued his job hunt while working at Intel, but now he could put the "Intel" at the top of his résumé instead of his graduate school experience. Ultimately, Illumina— a start-up firm specializing in human gene sequencing—offered William a full-time position because they liked the combination of his PhD training and his Intel experience. And as for William, he found that the culture of a start-up suited him well after the independence of graduate school and that his academic training is serving him well once again as he learns yet another new field.

So What's Next?

We hope that we've persuaded you in this chapter to slow down your job search and carefully research a handful of potential options instead of applying to every job opening you see. It may feel counterintuitive at first, but we promise that your results will be better. You'll find that you get more calls for interviews by applying for fewer jobs. And whether you seek the answers to the Big Questions by looking online, reaching out to your networking contacts, or taking on a volunteer gig, you will find that your job hunt is richer and more rewarding because you will be learning as you go. It's true that you won't see immediate results—you never know just when or how all your hard work will be rewarded, but we promise that it will be. Networking is not linear, but that doesn't mean it doesn't work. As Yale's Director of Graduate Career Services Victoria Blodgett reminded us, "Career searching is not something you turn on and off. You do it every day whether you realize it or not. When you talk to people about your work, about your passions, about what you're reading, about your field, you are building your network and building your experience." Be patient. Keep working at it. And you'll soon find yourself the beneficiary of your own self-created luck.

....

POST-ACADEMIC PROFILE:
XIUWEN TU, PHD IN PHYSICS, SUN POWER CORPORATION,
DEVICE AND CHARACTERIZATION ENGINEER

Xiuwen first began having concerns about the state of the academic job market in the final year of his physics PhD at University of California–Irvine. He had noticed that his friends who graduated before him were struggling to find tenure-track positions. Then he went to a seminar on the future of academic science where he heard a faculty member say that "a principal investigator might educate twenty graduate students his lifetime, but only one can replace him."

Instead of being discouraged, Xiuwen started thinking about what else interested him. Solar energy was a booming emerging industry at the time and had always intrigued him, so he started researching the field. He paid his own way to a solar energy conference in San Francisco and wandered from booth to booth, speaking to as many people as he could. He liked what he heard and decided to focus his search on solar energy.

There was just one catch: his dissertation research was all about the movement of atoms and molecules at extremely low temperatures. He was an expert in the *exact opposite* of solar energy. And he also knew from his research on the industry that an engineering background would be much more desirable to an employer than his more abstract physics degree. What could he do to prove his skills and his interest to an employer?

Xiuwen devised a brilliant solution. His advisor had asked him to do an outreach program for high school students: his task was to engage the students in a simple experiment appropriate for their level. So Xiuwen decided to use this opportunity to his advantage. He had the class build primitive solar cells using, oddly enough, blackberry juice. The experiment was a hit with the students and—informal as it was—it enabled him to prove to his interviewers that he was serious about a career in solar energy.

Xiuwen left nothing to chance, however, and prepared carefully for those interviews. "I had a basic foundation in semiconductor physics, but I knew that engineers would have more specialized knowledge so I reviewed the material in more detail to make sure I was ready." He also went to the UCI career center to "learn more about how to stand out and how to do better in interviews." He did a mock interview with a career counselor and also asked her to review his cover letter and résumé.

He finds his new position satisfying and fulfilling, he says, because he is now "solving real problems in the corporate world" instead of conducting fundamental research that has no practical application.

4 **This Might Hurt a Bit**

Turning a CV into a Résumé

It's not about you. It's about the job.

The biggest difference between a résumé and a curriculum vitae (CV) is that a résumé focuses on the employer's needs, rather than explaining every detail of your credentials. Every time we help someone turn a CV into a résumé (and when we struggled with it ourselves), our advice always boils down to the same essential point: Your résumé has to teach the reader why you can do *this particular job.* This change in approach may not sound that large to you right now, but, done correctly, the process requires a seismic shift. You'll have to learn to see yourself in an entirely different way.

Résumé writing is not pleasant work. No one likes to remove all those hard-won publications and conference papers from their CV or condense years of teaching experience into a single line. Downplaying your academic credentials feels like failure. So why can't you just reorganize your CV and let employers figure out the rest for themselves? They can see you're smart enough to do whatever they need done, right? Wrong.

In fact, if you're not speaking the employer's language, your résumé might never even be read. As Graduate Career Counselor at University of California–Irvine Christine Kelly says:

> Most firms use a computer system that screens résumés looking for keywords, and if you don't have the right words in your

résumé, it will never get to a human being. Now, I might be able to ferret out your meaning as we sit here together, but you need to translate your experience for the employer, explain it more clearly, and use their own language.

If everyone else submits résumés that speak directly to the employer's needs, why should he or she (or the résumé bot) spend extra time trying to puzzle out your credentials?

In addition, the range of candidates applying for any post-academic job is enormous compared to those who apply for academic jobs. For example, let's say that you're seeking a position as a postdoc or an assistant professor of biology. You know your competition well—other PhDs in the same field who have similar research and teaching experience. Your challenge in applying for this job is to make small differences in your intellectual approach stand out in a field of similar candidates.

Now imagine yourself applying for a job with a consulting firm specializing in environmental science. Sure, you have a PhD in biology that shows you're a smart cookie and you've been doing bench research for ages. Your science skills are transferrable but there is nothing on your résumé that reflects an interest in or experience with environmental science or experience working with clients. Why should an employer take the risk of hiring a person with zero experience? That's why your résumé has to be persuasive and relevant. You can't expect special treatment. You must reduce the risk of employing you by showing that you have done similar work before, that you have the relevant skills, that you understand the mission, and that you are eager to be a part of this group.

While all that may sound daunting, there is also some good news. First, your chance of getting the job is as good as anyone else's if you can make a convincing case for yourself. (We've heard occasional stories about people flatly refusing to interview or hire PhDs, and it does happen from time to time. However, we've seen far more PhDs ruin their own chances by submitting a seven-page résumé or talking endlessly about their dissertations in the interview.) Second, your research and teaching skills can give you an advantage in your job hunting. Third, a PhD after your name certainly helps your résumé get noticed. It also means that you can juggle evidence and construct an argument, which is exactly what you must do in your résumé and your cover letter.

Although we've said that you must show that you fit "this particular job," we don't mean that you have to contort yourself to fit the requirements of some vaguely interesting help-wanted ad. For now, your imagined audience should be any company or organization you've learned about through your research and networking.

Take note: It may take you several tries to develop a presentable résumé. Karen Rignall, a former graduate student in anthropology, recalls that her first attempts to turn her CV into a résumé were a bit misguided. "I looked back at my first résumé and it seemed so naive. I had made no effort to pare it down, to make it readable; even the font was hard to read. It looked like an academic paper and was clearly an academic talking, even though I was trying to stress the part-time jobs. It was wordy and looked awful visually."

For Rignall, the whole process of cataloging her achievements was gut-wrenching. Disheartened by several years of graduate study, her biggest problem was a lack of confidence. "I had a hard time accepting my accomplishments and conveying them in a résumé. It seemed immodest. I felt like I couldn't claim my earlier experiences: 'I don't really know how to do that.'" Eventually, a supportive friend who had left graduate school for the business world sat down and helped her present her achievements in an appropriate format, but the experience was still difficult. "She gave me good, constructive advice," Rignall recalls, "and I cried anyway."

At this stage it's especially important to reach out to the career counselors at your university if you haven't done so already. They'll be able to tell you what does and doesn't work, what kind of lingo you need to use, and how to present yourself in the best light. You should listen carefully to their advice as you begin drafting materials.

REAL-WORLD WRITING SAMPLES

It's common for employers in all kinds of fields to ask applicants to submit a writing sample with a résumé before an interview. Since you've poured your heart into your dissertation, you may be tempted to use it (or a related journal article) as evidence of your way with words. Don't do it. While your dissertation may be an example of your finest academic writing, it is absolutely not appropriate to use as a real-world writing sample. As Colleen Shogan, Deputy Director of the Congressional Research Service, explains, "Most employers will want to know whether you can write in a readable, nonacademic style."

Just as you had to learn the form of academic writing, you'll have to absorb the principles of post-academic writing in order to meet the employer's expectations. Most firms want to see a direct and concise style. Don't hesitate to ask an employer what they want to see in a writing sample, but don't be surprised if the answer is vague. Part of your job hunting research includes researching the audience for your writing sample, so turn to your network and career services counselors for help. Your sample should be as short as possible, usually no more than five pages. A little personality or humor in the writing can catch an employer's eye, but strive for clarity above all else. Avoid academic jargon.

So where do you get experience in this kind of writing? If you want to write as a career, try to publish some freelance articles for the local newspaper or the alumni magazine. Volunteer to be a guest blogger for an organization that matters to you, whether it's your local animal shelter or the food bank at which you volunteer. One academic told us that he prepared for a possible career change to journalism by writing occasional articles for *Runner's World* magazine. He was a serious distance runner and loved writing pieces on his favorite subject. Consider adapting this strategy to your own interests. Freelance writing rarely pays well, but building a portfolio of work can make it worthwhile.

Don't stop with journalism. Consider other types of writing like grant proposals to showcase your skills. If you're still in grad school, chances are good that your university's graduate student organization or your discipline's professional association or even your own department may award grants to support student programming or conference travel. Research grant writing online and do a great job with your proposal, even if it's for a small grant. Submitting this kind of results-oriented writing sample can make you stand out in the crowd.

What if you need a writing sample right away? It's okay to improvise. You need not submit published work so choose any format you find comfortable: opinion piece, magazine article, blog, or even Power Point slides. Your best bet, however, is to write about a topic related to the job you're seeking. Use your customized writing sample as another opportunity to strengthen the case for hiring you.

Amy Pszczolkowski, Graduate Career Counselor at Princeton, has helped countless graduate students convert their CVs to résumés and says that far too many rush the process. Candidates "just shorten the CV to one page without adapting the language or tailoring the content for the needs of the industry. If you haven't researched the industry, or don't have a specific job in mind, then you can't tailor effectively," she advises.

Getting Ready to Write a Résumé

You may have been so focused on the Big Three of the CV (scholarship, teaching, and service) for the past several years that you've forgotten why these categories exist in the first place: to please a particular audience. The Big Three are nothing more than a list of the qualities that are important to the committees that hire assistant professors. The Big Three do not define you. The Big Three are not your only skills. In fact, they may not even be your greatest strengths. Most grad students and professors are well aware that they are not equally gifted in all three areas. Let that knowledge free you from pretending to be someone you're not.

A better set of principles to keep in mind when creating your résumé is the Big Questions from chapter 3. Focus on what you have learned about the job, the organization, and the industry as a whole from your pursuit of the Big Questions when drafting your résumé. Doing so will ensure that you are demonstrating your understanding of the organization as well as speaking directly to the employer's priorities and concerns, which all adds up to a persuasive and compelling case for hiring you.

Reimagine Your Past

Graduate school may have taught you to be harshly critical of yourself. Is there such a thing as a happy, confident graduate

DOES A PHD MAKE ME OVERQUALIFIED?

One of the most frequent questions we're asked when we give talks to graduate students is: "Doesn't a PhD make me over-qualified?" Frustrated when they don't get interviews or offers, some job seekers assume that the PhD on their résumé is holding them back. Some wonder if they should omit the degree from their résumé entirely.

But here's the painful truth: it's much more likely that a PhD seeking a job outside academia is underqualified rather than overqualified. While a doctorate exceeds the educational qualifications for most jobs, that's not the most important measure of your candidacy. The employer is looking for relevant experience, and if you don't have it, your degree is irrelevant.

So what are you supposed to do? The good news is that all you need is a little bit of experience to tip the scales in your favor. A PhD is a great asset—it shows you are smart, hardworking, and highly capable. So if you can combine that experience with an internship, some volunteer work, anything that helps get your foot in the door, you will be a far stronger candidate, whether you are a PhD, A.B.D., or master's student.

student? It's time to learn to see yourself outside of the graduate school mold. Let's start with your past.

First, make a laundry list of every activity you've ever done, including summer jobs, internships, hobbies, volunteer work, part-time gigs, big academic or administrative projects, temp jobs, etc. Everything counts. Now, describe each event in as many ways as possible. How would you describe that job to your neighbor? To a stranger on the subway? Step back and try to get a broader view of what you've done.

Pick out the most interesting and relevant parts of the experience, and quantify whenever possible. How many people did you work with? What was the result of your work? How many months or years of experience did you gain? Did you have any ideas, however small, that made things work a little better around the office? What did you bring to the experience that the previous person did not? It may feel a little weird to highlight one detail of your summer job without contextualizing it alongside the rest of your duties, but that's actually a good sign that you're writing with your audience's needs in mind. Here are some examples:

- **Public speaking experience:** Delivered multimedia presentations to groups of 100+ weekly; developed strong ability to handle spontaneous Q&A while teaching college courses ranging from beginner to advanced level. (Notice that you don't need to name the courses or how many of them you taught.)
- **Project management:** Worked with team of ten writers to produce campus publication on weekly deadline. (Notice that you don't need to say what your title was or what the publication was.)
- **Leadership (or teamwork):** Led groups of high-school students on summer backpacking trips in the Adirondack Mountains. Worked with three other leaders to ensure safety of campers.
- **Computer skills:** Knowledge of [list program names here]. (Note that you don't have to say how well you know each one—if you've done any work at all with the program, that's enough.)

One of the biggest disadvantages that academics face in writing résumés is that they've been trained to be scrupulously exact. Résumés require a different frame of mind. No, we're not suggesting that you should lie on your résumé. But as the previous examples show, standards of proof are quite different outside the academy. In fact, most people would say that academic standards are bizarrely specific.

For example, your CV would carefully detail whether you were a teaching assistant, a lecturer, or an instructor, and you'd be sure to give the full title of every course that you've ever taught. But on your résumé, you need provide only a concise summary: "Taught college-level economics courses ranging from beginner to advanced levels." Your classes should not be enumerated, but characterized. The details just don't matter much outside the academy and spelling them out just shows that you don't quite get the conventions of the world beyond academia.

When you describe summer jobs or part-time work, you also need to be careful you don't sell yourself short. "But I was just a lowly summer intern at a museum," you say. Well, we'd bet that you learned a great deal about how museums work and probably contributed more than your title would indicate. Your résumé should reflect the best of that experience, not what your W-2 says about you. Try to let go of the insecurities about "expertise" that academia fosters. Your experiences do not need to be peer reviewed or formally vetted in order to be valid and meaningful. Take a kindly view of yourself, and you'll do a better job of presenting your true value and potential.

Once you've drafted a list of important experiences, make an appointment with a career counselor at your university who can help you brainstorm your way to a first draft.

Research Your Future

As you know from asking the Big Questions in chapter 3, you need to research your target employer extensively in order to write a persuasive résumé and cover letter. It's impossible to create a convincing argument without having a clear, specific thesis in mind. Think about those awful papers that English 101 students turn in with mind-bogglingly general theses like "Since the beginning of time, man has needed heroes." To a teacher who's trying to evaluate whether the student has understood *Wuthering Heights,* this paper doesn't look promising. Avoid that same pitfall in writing your résumé by knowing exactly whom you are trying to reach and what they want to hear from you.

The key is focusing on the challenges and obstacles each organization faces. That's what the Big Questions are all about: What do they need and how can you help? That means doing more than just reading their list of job openings. It means reading between the lines to find out as much as you can about a potential employer.

If it sounds like we're asking you to invest an awful lot of time before even writing the first line of your résumé, that's exactly right. Not only does advance research make your résumé more effective, but it helps you figure out whether this firm is really where you want to spend forty hours of your week. It's a waste of your time to apply to a company you don't know anything about, and your odds of success are much lower.

You can do this: you're an expert researcher. You just need to learn to shift from your dissertation topic to researching potential employers *before* you begin crafting a résumé. So if you skipped over the Big Questions in chapter 3 and have jumped ahead to drafting your résumé, please go back and review that section before you start writing. If you want to create a knockout résumé, you'll need to answer at least half of the Big Questions in chapter 3 before you start writing.

Finally, although we have been talking about "your résumé" as if it is a single document, what you should be seeking to create is a baseline résumé, which you will revise and adapt repeatedly in order to make sure you're submitting a highly tailored and job-specific résumé for each position you're pursuing. As you apply the knowledge gained from the Big Questions to each job application, you'll see new ways in which you can strengthen the case for yourself by highlighting one experience or skill over another in each new version of your materials.

Writing a Résumé: The First Draft

Despite what some résumé books may tell you, there's no one magic formula guaranteed to land you a position. The two most common formats for organizing résumés are reverse chronological and skills-based. You may find that your best bet is a hybrid of the two. Ultimately, the format you use should be dictated by the job to which you're applying and the kind of experience you have to offer. We recommend that you try out both formats to see the advantages and disadvantages of each.

Reverse Chronological Résumé

The reverse chronological résumé is the one most people know best. List your experience from most recent to least recent. The trick here is to focus on the events that will interest the employer, without breaking the timeline or leaving any odd-looking gaps.

Advantages: This style is great for someone whose current job is in the field that they want to enter. The reader will identify you largely by the first entry on your résumé, so make sure it represents you as you want to be seen. This format also lets you choose between emphasizing either the companies you've worked for (**The World Bank**, summer intern and coffee gofer) or the positions you've held (**Statistician**, Some Tiny Little Company Unrelated to Your Major Interest).

Disadvantages: The reverse chronological format can trip you up pretty quickly if the string of experiences that you want to present doesn't work chronologically. Maybe you're adjunct teaching right now, but you want to apply for a job that's not related to teaching. Check out our sample résumés to see how other alumni handled this situation. The bottom line is that your résumé should answer questions, not raise them. If it looks funny to you, it'll look even stranger to an employer.

Skills-Based Résumé

If you've had little direct experience in the industry or field you hope to join, it may be easier to sell yourself by translating your past jobs into concrete skills rather than focusing on the jobs themselves. Your company research is crucial here. What skills are important to them? What are the company's priorities? Then you can map your experience onto their framework.

Advantages: A skills-based résumé is much more accommodating for people who've had unusual career paths (actually, that includes just about everybody). You can also grab an employer's attention more quickly if your résumé spells out exactly the skills they're looking for.

Disadvantages: Too much freedom can be a bad thing. Be careful to make your résumé "show, not tell." If you're presenting yourself as having public relations skills, you should be able to give evidence of some relevant experience that doesn't require too much interpretation on the reader's part. Also, many a grad student has added subheadings for research and writing skills to their CV and called it a résumé. Don't fall into that trap.

Remember that you probably have a more diverse set of skills than you realize. Clinging exclusively to your academic achievements may keep you from discovering your other assets. For example, Margit Rankin, a PhD in comparative literature, had a difficult time removing her academic publications from her work history when she first starting looking at positions outside academia. She'd spent years laboring over these projects; it seemed unfair that they shouldn't be mentioned on her résumé. But since they weren't relevant to her search, they had to go. Once she condensed her academic achievements, she realized there was now room on her résumé to highlight some of the skills she had acquired during her many years of working off and on at her family's photography studio in Richmond, Virginia.

She remembers that while working at the studio, she "discovered a stash of hundreds of old hand-colored window samples—beautiful pieces of work." Inspired, she set to work:

I identified the portraits, researched our historical files, contacted the families, and placed an advertisement in the newspaper offering these photos for sale at an attractive price (just imagine a hand-painted picture of your wife or husband or mother—or grandfather—something that would cost hundreds or even thousands of dollars). We made a fair amount of money. These samples were simply gathering dust and would otherwise have been thrown away. They certainly would not have generated any income.

When incorporated into her résumé (and later described to employers during interviews), this informal experience showed how Rankin used creative problem-solving, research skills, and marketing savvy to increase the bottom line of a business.

A Few More Words of Advice

Experiment with profiles.

You might have seen résumés that have a "skill overview," "profile," or "career summary" statement at the top. They usually read something like "A manager with twelve years' experience seeking a challenging position in the hospitality industry." Should you try this approach? A good career statement can help you, but a bad one can hurt you, so you'll have to test-drive a few with your network of contacts in order to decide what works best for you (or if you need one at all).

The most effective career statements are concise, specific, and clearly focused. They should address the employer's needs (have we mentioned this before?) and clarify why you are the right person for the job. Try summarizing and emphasizing your relevant experience: Five years of experience in laboratory research? Six years of experience in student mentoring? Experienced researcher and writer with extensive knowledge of economics? If you don't have strong experience in the field you want to enter, you can at least highlight your interest and relevant skills here.

A word of caution: avoid vague, self-absorbed, and long-winded career statements at all costs. Listing as your objective "Seeking challenging position in an environmentally friendly company where I can grow and succeed" will sink an otherwise strong résumé. While that sentence may indeed describe exactly what you're looking for in a job, that's not the question your résumé needs to answer.

Keep your résumé to one page.
How, you may ask, can you distill all your years of education, original research, teaching, conference papers, mentoring, and scholarship onto one page? This is the wrong question. Remember, focus on your prospective employer, not on yourself. Chances are that the hiring manager who receives your résumé will spend about thirty seconds reading it—which means they'll never get to the second page. So make it short and easy to scan.

A lot of items that belong on a CV are redundant on a résumé. This may hurt a little, but here's a list of what *not* to include on your résumé:

- the title of your dissertation (just list your field of study)
- titles or descriptions of courses you've taught (summarize your experience in a short phrase: "three years teaching college-level biology")
- all the awards you've won as either an undergrad or a grad student (except maybe one or two biggies)
- your advisers' names
- your MA date if you earned your PhD at the same institution
- the conferences you've attended and/or papers you've presented
- the articles or books you've published, unless directly relevant to the job you want

Use capitalization, bold, *italics*, <u>underlining</u>, and white space.
Don't be afraid to highlight your strongest credentials with visual cues. Most of the CVs we've read (and sent out) have been pretty dry-looking documents—they list a candidate's education and dissertation at the top followed by a list of classes taught and articles published, all in tiny Times New Roman type. It's okay to make things a little more visually appealing outside the academy.

This doesn't mean that you should use a script typeface and pink paper. It's just to say that you can be a little more creative with the aesthetics of your résumé.

Try some new vocabulary.

Every résumé needs some active verbs to make it powerful. If it seems like the only verbs that describe your academic experience are "wrote" and "researched," try using some of the following to describe the breadth of your experience:

Achieved	Defined	Measured
Analyzed	Described	Mentored
Applied	Designed	Negotiated
Arranged	Developed	Organized
Assessed	Evaluated	Performed
Assisted	Excelled	Presented
Authored	Explained	Produced
Balanced	Explored	Proved
Built	Guided	Recruited
Calibrated	Hired	Researched
Cataloged	Identified	Reviewed
Coached	Illustrated	Shaped
Collaborated	Increased	Solved
Communicated	Initiated	Taught
Conducted	Introduced	Trained
Convinced	Invented	Won
Coordinated	Led	
Created	Managed	

Employers seek people with certain skills they believe are essential to a successful workforce. And you've developed many of these skills in graduate school, including communication skills (if you worked as a teaching assistant), analytical skills, and project management experience (you worked on a dissertation or thesis, right?), so be sure to highlight these on your résumé.

After You've Drafted a Résumé

Show it to your network.

It cost you some blood, sweat, and tears, but you've made a résumé. Now it's time to get it critiqued. It's crucial that you share your résumé with as many people in your network as possible (including the counselors at your university career services office). It will take quite a few tries to come up with an effective résumé, and you'll have to make alternate versions for different kinds of jobs or industries. But the more you work on your résumé, the more you'll learn about the field and about how to position yourself within it.

Case Studies and Sample Résumés

In this section, you'll find résumés created by people seeking their first full-time position outside academia. We've described the kind of jobs that each person was seeking so that you can see how they adapted their résumés to the employer's needs. We are grateful to all these alumni for letting us use their real-life résumés (some identifying details have been changed) for educational purposes.

Case Study #1: Thelma Tennant, PhD Biology: Reaching a Wider Audience

Thelma Tennant embarked on a career in science because she wanted to make a difference in the world. Earning a PhD in cancer biology with a dissertation on prostate cancer metastasis made a clear contribution not only to her field but also to mankind. Her philanthropic goals led her to continued research on leukemia as a postdoctoral scholar.

But while completing her postdoc, she had some key insights. She realized that despite her expertise, she was not in the top 5 percent of researchers in her field and only the top percent could ever hope to receive grants because of the erosion of federal

THELMA R. TENNANT, PHD
Chicago, IL 60615

EDUCATION

University of Chicago   Doctor of Philosophy in Cancer Biology
Chicago, IL, Dec. 20XX

University of Virginia   Bachelor of Arts in Biology (with Distinction)
and Bachelor of Arts in English
Charlottesville, VA, May 19XX

EXPERIENCE

Postdoctoral Scholar, University of Chicago, Chicago, IL, 20XX–20XX
"Chromosomal Abnormalities in Malignant Myeloid Disorders"

- Collaborated with five research groups across the country to identify karyotypic abnormalities associated with leukemia and lymphoma
- Surveyed and analyzed a large body of patient data to identify common abnormalities in patients with myeloid disease
- Used genomic profiling techniques, molecular methods, and cytogenetic analyses to examine candidate tumor-suppressor genes in therapy-related leukemias

Instructor and Teaching Assistant, Chicago, IL, 19XX–20XX

- Designed and implemented a ten-week course on teaching methods, classroom, strategies, and presentation skills for teaching assistants
- Led undergraduate class discussions, conducted study sections, assisted with test design, and graded all class assignments and exams

Program Assistant, Northeast Environmental Research Association, USDA, College Park, MD, 19XX–19XX

- Assisted in management of large-scale agricultural biotechnology research
- Developed an interactive web-based communication system for agricultural biotechnology risk assessment regulators

Program Assistant, USDA National Biotechnology Impact Assessment Program, Washington, D.C, 19XX–19XX

- Designed and implemented a searchable agricultural biotechnology research results database
- Managed grant program for agricultural biotechnology risk assessment

AWARDS

- Edward L. Kaplan New Venture Challenge, 1st Place, June 19XX
- Penikoff Foundation Fellowship for Prostate Cancer Research, Apr. 19XX–20XX
- University of Chicago Women's Board Foundation for Cancer Research Award, Oct. 19XX, 19XX Graduate Student Fellowship

PUBLICATIONS

John M. Joslin, Anthony A Fernald, **Thelma R. Tennant**, Elizabeth M. Davis, Scott C Kogan, John Anastasi, John D. Crispino, and Michelle M. Le Beau. "Haploinsufficiency of EGR1, a candidate gene in the del(5q), leads to the development of myeloid disorders." _Blood_. 2007 Jul 15;110(2):719-26.

Thelma R. Tennant, Courtney M.P. Hollowell, Mithra K. Zaucha, Erich B. Jaeger, Stacey R. Raviv, Walter M. Stadler, and Carrie W. Rinker-Schaeffer. "Upregulation of matrix metalloproteinase 2 during metastasis of prostate cancer cells." *In progress.*

Erich B. Jaeger, Marina A. Chekmareva, **Thelma R. Tennant,** Hue H. Luu, Jonathan A. Hickson, Steven L. Chen , R.S. Samant, Mitchell H. Sokoloff, and Carrie W. Rinker-Schaeffer. "Inhibition of prostate cancer metastatic colonization by approximately 4.2 Mb of human chromosome 12." *International Journal of Cancer.* 2004 Jan 1;108(1):15-22.

LEADERSHIP EXPERIENCE
Resident Head, Dodd Mead House, University of Chicago, Chicago, IL, 20XX–20XX
- Manage and supervise a 56-student undergraduate residence
- Provide counseling on academic and career-related topics and psychological concerns
- Plan and implement social programs, including community service activities

Co-Chair, Biological Sciences Division (BSD) Dean's Council, Chicago, IL
- Led organization in decision-making for the BSD graduate student body, 19XX–20XX
- Advised the Dean of Students regarding graduate student needs and concerns
- Allocated funds for student activities

INTERESTS
Sailing

funding. She also realized that she liked interacting with people, something that didn't happen enough in the lab.

"As my postdoctoral research began to wind down, I realized that I had become 'typecast' as a mouse researcher. I was good at handling mice, which is a valuable skill. However, I didn't want to spend the rest of my life in a mouse room, coming home each day smelling of mouse poo," she recalled. "And I also realized that I was not among the increasingly rarefied population of young researchers who were likely to score the necessary grants and funding that would help land a tier-one academic position."

Making the decision to seek post-academic employment was difficult, however, because she wanted to stay in science and she liked working at an elite institution "because the intellectual stimulation and high quality of the work was exciting and interesting." She began to explore other careers in patent law and corporate research. "I realized that my interpersonal skills were underutilized in my bench-work position, and because I enjoy working with people, I decided to look for a job that would allow me to flex both my scientific skills and my communication skills." A double major in biology and English as an undergraduate, she had established credentials in communications to go with her scientific knowledge. She met with an executive recruiter and began working on résumés and cover letters.

She also reached out to a network of friends she had met in the scientific community, including a former classmate who was working for UChicago Tech, the University's Office of Technology and Intellectual Property. When he heard about her search, he encouraged her to apply for an assistant project manager job with his office.

She learned that the office serves University of Chicago researchers by building the commercial potential of their ideas and inventions. It also works with industry to understand company and market needs and whether the intellectual capital at the University can help.

Thelma realized that such a position would allow her to use her scientific knowledge to reach a much larger audience than she had been able to reach as an academic researcher. "It was right where I wanted to be because I could get research out to the public," she realized. But first she had to convince the employer that she was right for the job. In order to prepare for the interview she adjusted her résumé to fit the requirements of the job by doing the following:

- **Stressed skills required for the job:** Thelma rewrote her résumé to highlight specific experience required in the new job. They needed a manager, so she stressed her work **managing** biotech research and **managing** a risk assessment grant program.
- **Included relevant publications:** We often advise graduate alumni to omit or at least limit the academic publications they include on their résumés, but Thelma's articles are appropriate because they are relevant to the position she sought. The position requires that she meet with senior faculty across the university, so it was important to showcase her scientific ex-

pertise. She created other versions of her résumé that deleted publications, but this was the **right résumé for this job.**

- **Featured evidence of her ability to work with diverse groups of people:** Bridging the divide between industry and academia requires well-developed interpersonal and communication skills. Thelma highlights her work as a head of a college residence hall, explaining, "I was a resident head in a dorm for eleven years, and the interpersonal skills I developed in that position were of great interest and value to my current employer."

- **Added hobbies and interests:** When Thelma interviewed, she was surprised that the interviewer spent more time asking about her interest in sailing than any other line on her résumé. It turns out that he was an avid sailor who sailed the same type of boats that Thelma favored. You can't be certain that you'll share a hobby with your interviewer, but you can prepare answers about your hobbies that highlight desired qualities for a job (in Thelma's case, she was able to present herself as an experienced crew member).

Thelma now finds great satisfaction in bringing university research to a larger audience. She credits her success to connecting her scholarly expertise with her other interests and talents. Featuring your experience outside the lab on a résumé "is not to say that your graduate degree is not valuable," she advises other job seekers, "but presenting (and thinking carefully about) you as the whole package can distinguish you from the rest."

Case Study #2: Howard Jones, A.B.D. English: How to Make Part-Time Work Add Up to Full-Time Experience

Howard Jones always knew that he wanted to earn a doctorate. "I was laser focused on going to grad school from my freshman year in college. I knew I wanted to get my PhD. My mom has a high school education, and my dad has an MBA but was first in his family to get a college degree." After having imagined himself as a

HOWARD JONES
Irvine, CA 92617
howard.jones@gmail.com
(949) 555-5555

Profile

- Versatile marketing professional specializing in copywriting, media planning, and building professional relationships.

Experience

Intern, February 20XX–Present
Xcellent Advertising, Huntington Beach, CA

- Wrote original radio scripts airing nationwide on SiriusXM. Revised existing marketing copy for website and sales brochures. Composed new articles for company blog. Increased click-through rate (CTR) on Google AdWord campaign from 0.07% to 6.74%.
- Assisted on the purchase of $40,000 worth of radio media monthly. Researched station demographics. Contacted and negotiated with sales reps. Analyzed schedules with Strata media buying software. Prepared Keynote presentations updating clients on campaign performance.
- Monitored media and trade serials to generate sales leads. Initiated contact with potential clients through cold calls and emails. Maintained contact records with Sage ACT! software.

PhD Student and Instructor, 20XX–20XX
School of Humanities, University of California, Irvine

- Provided timely, detail-oriented feedback on up to 500 total pages of undergraduate writing per three-month period. Edited and proofread graduate research projects (up to 50 pages each).
- Developed presentations, speeches, handouts, and activities to clearly communicate knowledge and guidelines. Achieved superior scores in each aspect of standardized evaluation.
- Independently synthesized complex information into insightful written commentary, ranging from one to 30 pages per project. Adapted messages to reach diverse audiences. Delivered on deadline.

Sales Assistant, September 20XX–August 20XX
Bob's Disposal & Recycling Services, Fallbrook, IL

- Facilitated communications between mobile sales team, garage facilities, and main office. Provided internal support for resolving scheduling and supply chain challenges between departments.
- Drafted letters regarding contract enforcement and price increases. Prepared contracts.
- Provided effective and efficient customer support in fast-paced environment. Assumed primary fleet dispatcher and receptionist duties in relief of staff.

New Student Programs Coordinator, 20XX–20XX
Office of the Dean of Students, University of Illinois at Urbana-Champaign
• Collaborated to organize 50 hours of PR training for 31 employees. Managed 10-member team.
• Collaborated to write and revise informational handouts distributed to 20,000 total attendees.
• Delivered introductory presentations to new students and parents (100 to 800 per audience).

Education

University of California, Irvine, June 20XX; MA, English
University of Illinois at Urbana-Champaign, May 20XX; BA, English and Philosophy

Technical Skills

• Microsoft Office (Word, Excel, PowerPoint, and Outlook) on Windows and Mac.
• Adobe Creative Suite 5.5 (Photoshop, Illustrator, Dreamweaver, etc.) and DSLR operation.
• Content management systems (Wordpress, Blogger, Tumblr, etc.). Familiar with HTML.

PhD for so long, it was difficult for Jones to reinvent himself and decide to leave the PhD program at the University of California–Irvine before completing the doctorate.

Like many classmates, he knew about the tough job market for PhDs, but "it wasn't real to me. It only seemed real when I was in the program and saw friends who were a few years ahead of me on the market having no luck at all."

After deciding that he would leave after the MA, Howard had to decide what to do next and figure out how to get hired with very little experience outside the academy. He thought he might try advertising or marketing but found no success after sending out stacks of résumés. A graduate career counselor at UC–Irvine suggested that an internship might help him convince an employer that his graduate studies in English were relevant to a career in marketing.

"I went to a career night at UCI for students interested in marketing and advertising. It was oriented more toward undergrads. I think a lot of graduate students are reluctant to go to a networking event where it's nearly all undergraduates, but I think you have to just do it," he explains. "I remember seeing that two of the recruiters were students I had taught in my first year as a graduate assistant four years ago. That was a tough moment, handing over my résumé to someone whose papers I was grading a few months ago."

But he also he met the owner of an advertising agency at the career fair, who suggested that he send a résumé for an internship. Being willing to swallow his pride and complete an internship was a critical step in his career transition, as it gave him the initial experience he needed to land a full-time job in advertising shortly afterward.

Here are the résumé strategies that helped him land the job:

- **He built experience by starting at a small firm:** Howard started with an unpaid, part-time internship at a small agency, which was an ideal place to build his skills. "There were lots of different things to do. I did copywriting for the web, for videos. I got to do market analysis, make up Powerpoints of market data for prospective clients, and that was the key to getting my new, full-time job. My new job is all about preparing client information."
- **He highlighted his other job experiences,** including his work at a recycling firm he did between college and graduate school. While this was not primarily an advertising and communications job, he highlights the aspects of the work most relevant to the marketing industry. In addition, his part-time work as a New Student Program Coordinator allows him to showcase the written and oral communication skills that are essential in his new job.
- **In describing his teaching experience,** Howard lists only the general topic of the classes he taught rather than exact titles and semesters.

A key lesson to be learned from Howard's story is that the attitude that you bring to your career transition is a key factor in your success. Because he brought an open mind, a lack of ego, and a readiness to learn to his exploration of the advertising world, doors opened up for him, leading first to his internship and later to his full-time position.

Cover Letters That Will Get You Hired

Now that you've spent an enormous amount of time polishing your résumé, you might be tempted to dash off a cover letter in no time flat. Resist the temptation. The cover letter will be the first thing that your prospective employer sees and can absolutely determine whether you get an interview.

Like résumés, these letters should to be customized to fit specific jobs. Amy Pszczolkowski, Graduate Career Counselor at Princeton, warns that some grad students "imagine you can have one cover letter for any management consulting job and don't realize that all consulting firms are different."

There are entire books devoted to the art of writing the perfect cover letter. We've adopted a slightly heretical approach, so you may want to check out some of those other books for more detail on the subject. Our wisdom boils down to one sentence: Keep it short and simple. You'll keep yourself out of trouble, and the employer will thank you for not wasting his or her time.

Most cover letters for academic appointments devote the better part of two single-spaced pages to explaining a dissertation topic, a philosophy of teaching, and so on. Cover letters for post-academic jobs, however, should be less than a page and should not mention your dissertation. Instead, highlight one or two key pieces of experience that show you're qualified for the job.

The goal of your cover letter should be to convey your enthusiasm for a particular job and give your best explanation of why you are well-suited for the position. As with the résumé, your focus should be on why you can do the job, not your life story. Don't talk about why you're thinking of leaving academia or how conflicted you are about the decision. Instead, say what interests you about the job and what experience makes you qualified to fill it.

Here's a basic outline to follow:

- **First paragraph:** Introduce yourself and express your interest in the job.
- **Second paragraph:** Highlight two or three particularly relevant pieces of experience that you know, based on your research into the Big Questions (you did read chapter 3, right?), will be of interest to the employer.
- **Third paragraph:** Close by saying that you'll follow up within a week.

As you develop your cover letter, **keep your language simple and direct.** Write in a style that feels natural to you. Imagine that you're speaking on the phone to someone you respect. Try to sound confident and clear, not stilted. Would you use phrases like "Thank you in advance for your anticipated cooperation" or "Please find my résumé enclosed for your perusal"? Substituting language such as "Thank you for your time" or "My résumé is enclosed for your review" will do just fine.

Attempting to sound somewhat friendly (or at least human) is a good goal, **but don't go overboard with humor or informality.** Another extreme to avoid is obsequiousness. Employers are not impressed when you try to flatter them about their "exciting opportunity at a remarkable company." Use specific examples to explain why you are excited about working for this firm, and avoid empty compliments.

If at all possible, **send your letter to a human being rather than "to whom it may concern."** Even though more and more companies now require candidates to submit materials through online application systems, don't forget that you are writing to specific people. Search the company website or call the main number to ask who the hiring manager for a particular position is and address your letter accordingly. If you have a personal contact, by all means mention it. Even if you have only the slightest connection with the recipient of your letter, highlight it: "I really enjoyed hearing you speak at the recent University of Maryland Graduate Career Forum. Your description of the varied tasks required of

Program Associates convinced me that I would be well-suited for the position."

Finally, proofread. Then proofread again. Get someone else to proofread for you. Then proofread again. Wait twenty-four hours and proofread again. Nothing will send your materials to the trash can faster than typographical errors.

Here is a sample letter to get you started:

Ms. Sarah Barton
The Nature Conservancy
4245 North Fairfax Drive, Suite 100
Arlington, VA 22203-1606

Dear Ms. Barton,

Clara Jones suggested that I contact you about the Conservation Planner position advertised on your website. My combination of communication and technical skills, outdoor experience, and leadership makes me a good fit for the Nature Conservancy. I am extremely interested in this position because I believe in the organization's mission of protecting lands while promoting good science.

While completing my master's in environmental science at Oregon State, I gained a variety of experiences that are relevant to this position. As an experienced teacher, I am well prepared for a job that requires diplomatic and effective communication with diverse public audiences. I also sharpened my technical skills during my graduate program through hands-on research using Geographic Information Systems (GIS). Finally, I understand that this position requires physical exertion and travel to remote areas and so am confident that my Certification in Wilderness First Aid and experience as an Outdoor Educator at the National Outdoor Leadership School (NOLS) will serve me well.

I look forward to speaking with you soon and will follow up with you in a few weeks to ensure you received my résumé.

Sincerely,
Sam Sweeney

This letter works because it begins with a personal contact, shows an understanding of the organization, and responds directly to the employer's needs (through research, the candidate learned that the Nature Conservancy wanted someone with strong communication skills, outdoor experience, diplomacy, and technical knowledge, including GIS). While every cover letter is unique, strive for a clear, conversational approach that clarifies your skills and illustrates how they match up with the job you seek.

Applying for jobs can be horribly nerve-racking. We've outlined the steps as if it's a simple 1-2-3 process, but we know that it just isn't that easy. While you're going through this process, seek out a buddy who can share the stress with you. Proofread each other's letters, cheer each other's successes, and boo each other's rejections. Every job hunter needs a friend.

POST-ACADEMIC PROFILE:
ALYSSA PICARD, PHD IN HISTORY, STAFF REPRESENTATIVE
FOR THE MICHIGAN AFFILIATE OF THE AMERICAN FEDERATION
OF TEACHERS

The field of labor organizing often appeals to PhDs who have sought to improve working conditions on their own campuses. Alyssa Picard turned that interest into a job. After earning her PhD in history at the University of Michigan, where she was active in the graduate employee union, she became a labor negotiator and organizer for the Michigan state affiliate of the American Federation of Teachers (AFT).

"Graduate school at Michigan politicized me. I was there while the university's affirmative-action policies were litigated. Partly because of the cases, I was becoming more aware of the racial segregation and broader inequity of opportunity that exist in the U.S. educational system and of the need for affirmative action as a remedy for those things," she explained.

She went through the academic job cycle twice and landed an on-campus interview. "I didn't try to hide my politics, but I hadn't considered them relevant to my candidacy. The interviewers there clearly knew about my activism (I assume they Googled me) and seemed really nervous about it," she recalled. "I had the distinct impression that if I repudiated my labor activism, I would have been offered the job. But the idea that I'd spent so many years in school to prepare for a job where I would have to hide or apologize for my deepest convictions really disgusted me. Fortunately, I had already been offered this job (with AFT), and I decided to accept it while I was waiting for the plane home from that interview."

The union job offer came as a result of the hard work she had done as a graduate student representative, which included acting as the lead negotiator in contract negotiations. Impressed with her work, the staff representative for the Michigan AFT encouraged her to apply for the job that she eventually accepted.

Increasing numbers of academics have become interested in labor organizing as they have joined unions at their own universities. "If you became an academic because you enjoyed solitude and time for writing and reflection, a job in labor organizing would not be a good fit. But if you became an academic because you enjoy teaching and the opportunity to discuss ideas, and if you are also passionate about questions of justice and resource allocation, you might really enjoy this work," she advises. "I probably do more of the kind of teaching I really like in this job than I ever did in a classroom." She encourages students considering such a career to get active in their local union (or to organize one if none exists).

Her calendar is a full one. "One key difference between this work and academic work has to do with working hours. I have a lot of control over my schedule, and most of my work takes place within standard business hours, but I have to be available for work tasks twenty-four hours a day, seven days a week. Typically, I am traveling, in meetings, or answering e-mail between 9 a.m. and 9 p.m. five days a week, and on weekends four or five times a year." Despite her busy schedule, Picard still finds time for scholarship, including publishing her book *Making the American Mouth: Dentists and Public Health in the Twentieth Century* with Rutgers University Press.

5 Sweaty Palms, Warm Heart

How to Turn an Interview into a Job

"Nothing that you've learned about how to get jobs in the academy will help you find a job in the real world," says Carol Barash, a former professor of eighteenth-century literature at Rutgers who now runs her own writing coaching company. She's quick to add that the skills she acquired as a graduate student and professor have been essential to her success in the business world but that she needed to unlearn the lessons of the academic job-hunting process before searching for a job in business. "The academic search is so passive. I mean, in what other career search in the world are you supposed to send out a bunch of résumés and just wait for the phone to ring?"

If you've been trained to conduct an academic job search, you may think of the job interview as the most passive stage of the process. You just sit there while the interviewer asks you questions about your strengths and weaknesses, your greatest accomplishment, and your five-year plan, right? And you don't need to do much research in advance because you can just ask your questions at the interview, right? Wrong. When you're applying for jobs outside the academy, the interview is your chance to show that you can do the job. Let's restate that: Your goal in the interview is to prove that you can do the job. You need to lower the risk of hiring you. Companies lose money on new employees at first because they have to train them, so they want to make sure they choose well. Remember how we said that the résumé is about them, not you? It's the same principle in the interview process.

Luckily, you have a secret weapon: the Big Questions from chapter 3. Just as your efforts to answer the Big Questions helped you draft a hard-to-resist résumé in chapter 4, those same insights will give you an enormous advantage as you prepare for an interview. The more you know about the organization, the more comfortable you'll be and the more smoothly your interview will go. And the more you know about the organization to which you're applying, the more powerful an impression you will make. Maybe this all sounds like basic advice to you, but it's amazing how few people take the time to do even the most basic research before an interview. And if you've been exploring the Big Questions since before you drafted your résumé, you'll find that you are far ahead of the crowd.

Of course, the interview is also the time for you to decide if this is a job you'd actually want to have. While it's flattering to be invited for a "real world" interview after years in graduate school, don't make the mistake of thinking that you'll be lucky to have any job they offer. As one happily placed alum told us, "If I did it all over again, I'd remember that I'm supposed to be interviewing them as much as they are interviewing me." You may be in for an unpleasant surprise down the road if you rush to accept a job without thinking about whether you can see yourself being happy and successful in that new environment.

In this chapter, we will show you how to do your best before, during, and after an interview. While our advice may not be that different from what you'll find in other career guides, we've tried to focus on the aspects of interviewing about which grad students ask us most.

Before the Interview

So you've checked your phone and e-mail constantly for the last two weeks and finally gotten that call you wanted: the company of your dreams wants you to come in for an interview. Fantastic! What do you do first? Begin by calling back the person who contacted you and ask everything you forgot to ask before: Who will I meet? How long will the interviews be? Is there a particular interview format they like to use, such as case-method questions? Hands-on trials? Written test? Prepared presentation? These questions will let you know what to expect and allow you to prepare appropriately. But these questions are only the beginning.

Schedule a pre-interview consultation with career services.

Your university's career services office is the perfect place to start your interview preparation. The staff knows what employers are seeking and will be able to conduct a mock interview with you and give you reliable feedback. If you have the option to have your mock interview captured on video, take it: the chance to see how you look to others and get helpful critiques from a career counselor is hugely valuable, and well worth the initial squeamishness you may feel. A practice interview (or two or three) will also help you feel less nervous about the real thing.

Victoria Blodgett, Director of Graduate Career Services at Yale, reports that the number one complaint she hears from employers who have interviewed graduate students is that they aren't adequately prepared. "I think very bright advanced degree students tend to be forward looking. They don't like to look backward," she reports. In addition to advising students to do their research on the organization (a.k.a answering the Big Questions), Blodgett encourages them to think about their own strengths and experiences: "What skills have I developed? What have others told me I do well? What experiences have I had that are evidence that I can use to persuade an employer?" Talking about yourself takes practice, so give yourself the advantage of trying out your stories on an experienced ear.

Reach out to your network and ask specific questions in order to prepare for the interview.

As you've been working to learn more about this job or industry, you should have made some connections along the way. Was there someone you spoke to or traded e-mails with who was particularly helpful and friendly? Now's the time to circle back and see if they might have additional insights to share. Let them know that you have an interview coming up and are continuing your research. You're now much better informed (right?) than when you first talked to this person, so here's an opportunity to take your questions to a new level and test out whether your perceptions of what the organization is seeking are accurate.

Practice your two-minute introduction.

You will need to be able summarize who you are and what you can do for this employer in a compelling two-minute introduction. While a two-minute pitch is also important in networking, in this case you're preparing for the interviewer who was unceremoniously pulled from his or her desk, dragged into the conference room, and handed your résumé. It happens all the time. In most offices, only one of the five or so people who may interview you has actually read your résumé in advance. Be prepared to make it easy for the people who are starting cold. Don't assume they know what you just told someone else. You need to supply these people with the rationale they'll need when someone asks them, "So, what did you think of him/her?" Your two-minute pitch serves this important purpose by neatly summarizing your skills and experience in terms that are meaningful to the employer.

Prepare for standard kinds of interview questions.

Standard human resources screening questions include: What's your greatest strength? Worst fault? Do you prefer to work in a team or by yourself? How do you handle disappointment? Where do you see yourself in five years? You can easily find career guides with long lists of these questions and examples of good and bad answers. It can be helpful to consult these lists and get familiar with some of the most common questions. But don't try to memorize these lists—this isn't the GRE. There are three key points to remember about answering any interview question:

1. Always speak positively about yourself.
2. Use specific examples to make a point.
3. Frame your answers toward the requirements of the job, rather than getting tangled up in an analysis of your personality.

For example, if you know that the job requires keeping a team project on schedule, you can say, "I'm a deadline-driven person, so I sometimes get frustrated by procrastinators. But I know that everyone has their own strengths and weaknesses to contribute. Here's an example: I collaborated on an article with a colleague who was terrible about meeting deadlines. But she was very creative and full of good ideas, so we each gave a little, and together we produced a top-notch article. It was a great experience, and from what I understand, that kind of teamwork is important in this job too."

Whatever you do, keep your answers relatively brief and concise. Richard Bolles—the author of *What Color Is Your Parachute?*—has found that the ideal response time to interview questions can be anywhere from twenty seconds to two minutes. Those of us used to writing 300-page dissertations may have trouble confining ourselves to this limit, so concentrate on keeping it simple. Allow for give-and-take, with room for follow-up questions to elicit more detail as needed.

And a final important note: Remember that you should not discuss salary until you have a written job offer in hand. If an interviewer asks you about your salary requirements or history, do not respond with specific numbers. No matter how much they persist that they need a dollar figure, simply reassure them in a warm and friendly tone: "I'm very interested in working here, but I'm just not comfortable discussing salary at this point. I'm sure we'll be able to work out a salary that's agreeable to both of us when the time comes."

Prepare for a non-traditional interview format, if applicable.
Some industries like to move beyond standard interview questions to more surprising methods, like problem-solving exercises,

ADVICE FOR INTERNATIONAL STUDENTS

Job hunting can be daunting for any graduate student, but international graduate students face a particular set of challenges on the post-academic market. As Alfreda James, Graduate Career Counselor at Stony Brook University (and a PhD in American History) observes, "International students, having managed to survive/thrive in a different culture and language, may still struggle with the social and emotional aspects of career development."

The advice we offer throughout the book about exploring options, building a network, seeking out internships, and crafting résumés and cover letters applies to all job searchers, but international students need to manage additional requirements. None of these issues can be addressed quickly, so it's important to start thinking about them early in your graduate career. Work with graduate career counselors and international student advisors at your university to chart your course.

Know the law.

Learn about the immigration laws and regulations that affect your employment eligibility before starting your search. You've likely already had to verify your employment status and eligibility based on your visa if you've held even a work-study position or fellowship as part of your graduate program. But your status can change once you complete the degree, so be sure to verify details. The more you know about the regulations, the better able you will be to negotiate with potential employers. International students "should learn how to explain their immigration status and be comfortable with it—this will reassure employers," advises Rachel Rubin, Director of International Services at Georgetown University. "They should learn how to put the cost of the H1B visa in perspective for employers—to see it as a simple recruiting cost and not a burden," she adds.

Refine your communication skills.

Some international graduate students may need additional language training to reach the level that employers demand. Because written and oral communication skills take time to develop, take advantage of the resources available at your university from the moment you arrive on campus. Seek out writing centers, language labs, and additional classes early in your graduate career to give yourself time to develop. If your native language is Chinese, for example, you might go to the department of Asian Studies and ask to be matched with a native English speaker who is studying Chinese. Having a regular conversation partner is an excellent way to build your language skills.

Consider cultural norms.
The cultural norms of life outside academia baffle many graduate students and may seem even stranger to someone from another country. "Many international students are not good networkers. They don't understand how to do it, they don't like to brag about themselves and are uncomfortable with the whole process," observes Rubin. In addition to networking, there are other aspects of job hunting, like writing résumés and covers letters and interviewing, that may feel like bragging. Again, career services can help you learn the conventions and become more comfortable with these activities.

Build a support group.
When he was looking for his first job as a management consultant, Shaohua Zhou met regularly with a small group of other Chinese PhDs in the sciences who were looking to make the same switch, he told us. They shared ideas, compared notes, and supported each other. After two years, Zhou said, everyone in the group who persisted in their search landed a job in consulting.

employment tests, or case-management questions. Use your contacts to try to figure out in advance what kinds of things you'll be asked. Candidates for consulting jobs just might not be able to get away from questions like, "How many taxis are there in Manhattan?" Happily, there are dozens of resources online and in your career center that can help you prepare for these kinds of questions. Make sure you learn and practice these strategies well in advance of your interview.

Some interviewers may spring completely off-the-wall questions on you. Jeff Bezos, founder of Amazon, likes to ask potential employees, "How would you design a car for deaf people?" Case-management techniques can help here too, but practicing how to stay calm and work out reasonable answers on the spot is probably the best approach. These kinds of questions usually don't have right or wrong answers. What the employers wants to see is how you analyze problems, how you work under pressure, and whether you can relate your answers to the job at hand.

Your graduate training gives you both an advantage and a disadvantage in these case-management/off-the-wall situations. On the one hand, you're well-prepared to answer the question: you've been taught to get to the heart of a problem, so draw on that skill and do your best. On the other hand, your graduate training may make you too cautious. This isn't academia; you can't go research the problem for six months before you give an answer. Don't worry about finding the perfect answer—make your best guess.

Make your own list of questions.
Interviewers will inevitably ask if you have any questions of your own, and you should be prepared with a thoughtful and carefully curated list. Your questions should reflect your high level of knowledge about the organization and give your interviewer some insight into how you would begin to approach the work.

Here are some sample questions you might ask:

- What are the biggest challenges you face in your position?
- What are some ways you address those challenges?
- How could the person you hire help solve these challenges?
- What do you see as the greatest threats/opportunities for this organization as a whole in the next 10 years?

Show your knowledge of the organization in your response to whatever they say and try to start a dialogue with your interviewer. These questions will help you start off a discussion about what needs to be done and how you can help, which is exactly the tone you want your interview to take. Of course you will also have more personal questions on your mind, about the culture of the company and nature of your role, but ask them sparingly or save those for a later interview. While it's true you should be evaluating them as much as they are evaluating you, keep the focus on the big picture needs of the organization at first. If they are interested in you, there will be plenty of time to ask your other questions along the way.

Get ready to teach someone how to read your résumé.
Here's where all those years of teaching undergraduate sections of Bio 101 or Intro to Art History will come in handy. We mentioned earlier that some of your interviewers are likely to have been yanked from their desks only moments before meeting you. They've just been handed your résumé on the way down the hall, and they never got to see that cover letter you worked so hard to get just right. In most cases, these interviewers are people who won't be working directly with you (so they're not too engaged in the whole process), but the hiring manager is still going to ask their opinion of your value. These interviewers can be a tough audience. But you can handle these kinds of interviewers skillfully if you realize in advance that they will probably be relying heavily on your résumé to guide their questions. So if you practice talking about the items on your résumé in a way that highlights the relevant points, you can teach them to see you as a person with valuable skills and experience.

Here's an example:

Interviewer, glancing at your résumé: "Hmmm . . . so what's the Jubilee Theater Group?" (What s/he means is: "What on earth does that have to do with this job?")

Weak answer: "Well, they put on lots of productions on campus; they do kind of avant-garde stuff compared to the more traditional theater groups. Last year they did a version of West Side Story set in Nazi Germany that was just amazing."

Strong answer: "It's a campus theater group—I was stage manager for three years. I was responsible for coordinating all the technical elements of our shows, ensuring that all the equipment worked correctly and that we hit all the technical cues. It was a great experience and taught me a lot about project management and grace under pressure."

Practice translating each item on your résumé into an example that will be valuable to the person sitting in front of you. Having thought through these connections in advance ensures that you'll instinctively make them during the interview even if you're never directly asked to do so.

During the Interview

Here you are in your best (read: only) suit, sitting alone in a huge conference room with a cup of lukewarm coffee, waiting for your first inquisitor. The person enters, shakes your hand, and you sit down again, wiping your sweaty palm on your knee. How do you stay calm? Nick Corcodilos has some great advice on this subject: "Start your meeting by making the interviewer talk. Most interviewers allow time at the start of an interview for idle chat. They're trying to relax you. Take advantage of this. Don't wait for the employer to ask the first question." An easy way to start is by asking your interviewer how long they've been with the company and what s/he does. Getting your interviewer to talk about his or her role will give you a chance to relax as well as offering some insights that can help shape your answers later in the interview. It's also never a bad idea to let someone talk about themselves.

Another tactic that can guide you during the interview is to draw upon your experience in the classroom. A good teacher is confident and knowledgeable, but also interested in what others have to say. Geoff Davis, a PhD in mathematics and a former professor at Dartmouth, found his teaching skills invaluable in landing a position at Microsoft. "One of the standard things in Microsoft interviews is that they send you to the board to solve problems, usually some kind of brain-teaser. The idea is to see how people think on their feet, and for most of their recruits, it's an unnerving and difficult situation. After teaching for four years, though, it was pretty easy for me. Put a piece of chalk in my hand and it's my show!"

Whatever you do, be confident and be clear—even if you're bluffing. Woody Allen once said that 80 percent of life is just showing up. We'd say that 80 percent of interviewing is believing in your own value. For an employer to see all you have to offer, you must first be convinced of it yourself. As with most things in life, an open mind and a positive attitude will carry you a long way.

Overcoming Stereotypes about PhDs

While a PhD on your résumé can get you noticed by a potential employer, it may also prompt an interviewer to assume that you are an absent-minded academic. Jennifer Scott knows all about these stereotypes because she's a former graduate student in early modern history at Columbia. One of the duties in her role as a senior producer/content manager for Morningside Ventures (now called Digital Knowledge Ventures), Columbia University's for-profit digital media company, was to recruit and interview new employees. Here are a few of her tips for handling negative perceptions of PhDs:

Academics aren't sufficiently focused on producing results.

PhDs have a reputation for "belaboring a point to its logical (or illogical) conclusion," Scott says. We're taught to argue, criticize, deconstruct, and to "debate for the sake of debate."

What she would like to see academics do in interview situations is "to show evidence of moving forward," to demonstrate that they can produce results rather than simply discuss a problem. A philosophy student we interviewed for this book shared a great example of this principle in action. Frustrated that his department provided little to no teaching training for graduate students, he asked his chair for permission to organize a semester-long workshop for new teaching assistants. The chair was more than happy to have someone else do the work, and the workshop was a huge success with his grateful fellow students. While his primary goal at the time was to improve the state of pedagogy in his department, he unintentionally gave himself a great story to tell at future job interviews.

Academics can't work in teams.

For some, pursuing a PhD can be a supremely solitary pursuit. Sure, you may do some teaching, but producing a dissertation requires that you spend countless hours working mostly alone in a library or lab. Be prepared to give "some evidence that you can work with others," advises Scott. Did you supervise other lab assistants? Jointly author articles? Plan a symposium? Be prepared with details and examples. Volunteer work and hobbies are fair game here and may actually provide even better answers than examples from your academic life.

Academics aren't risk-takers.

"Academic work is very measured," Scott says. "You're used to doing all the research before you say anything. In the digital world you have to get comfortable moving ahead with much less information."

Most of the questions you'll be asked in interviews don't have wrong answers. Many times the interviewer just wants to see how you think and react to new information. Interviewers expect you to have researched the organization and understand its mission, but they don't expect you to be an expert. So go ahead, hazard a guess. In many businesses it's better to be a little wrong than to be so cautious that you can't act.

You shouldn't worry too much about these stereotypes, for they are easily overcome with evidence of your success in non-academic endeavors. Ultimately, your chances as a PhD of being hired are as good, or better, than anyone else's. Also, these issues are only raised in connection to a PhD's first post-academic job—

once you've got some experience working outside academia, no one will bother you with these kinds of questions again.

What Should I Say about Graduate School?

You'll learn a lot about your interviewer from how they react to the graduate education listed on your résumé. Don't assume that one person's reaction will hold true for the rest of the company. Alumni have reported encountering these reactions:

- "Why do I need someone with all that education?"
- "I thought about going to grad school, but I didn't get in."
- "Why did it take so long for you to finish?" Or "Why didn't you finish?"
- "Gosh, you must be really smart." Or "I'd better watch my grammar."
- "Why would you want to work here?"
- "My brother-in-law has a PhD—I never understood why any- one would go to all that trouble."
- "Are you just killing time until next year? Do you plan to go on the market again?"

Academic credentials impress many people. But in rare cases they can also make some folks hostile or suspicious. Be prepared to make graceful, concise, and upbeat comments about your grad school experience. Maybe your feelings are still a little raw; maybe you plan to go on the market again next year. Don't talk about that during the interview. Just speak about the overall experi- ence as a challenge that you met successfully, and one in which you learned a great many skills that you'd like to apply in a new context. You've become an expert in one field—there's no reason why you can't become just as proficient in another. So you left in the middle of your program? That's nothing to be ashamed of. Most people have never been enrolled in a graduate program, so they should have no trouble understanding why you left.

Don't feel that you have to spill all the gory details; your interviewer is far less interested in this topic than you think s/he is. What the interviewer is really doing is testing your reaction. Do you seem to be torn or anxious about leaving academia? Are you likely to leave this job after a year? That's what they really want to know. Be concise and selective in your response. It's extremely common for alums who haven't yet made peace with their decision to talk nonstop for fifteen minutes about departmental politics when asked why they want to leave academia. Unfortunately, these kinds of angst-ridden responses are a sure way to knock yourself out of the running for any job.

Weak Answers:
- "I've been on the market five times, and I've been an adjunct for three years. There just aren't any tenure-track jobs out there."
- "My dissertation topic just wasn't fashionable enough for the job market. There are a lot of politics around who gets hired these days."
- "It's really hard to get funding for basic scientific research and there aren't many tenure-track jobs."
- "Well, I don't really want to leave academia, but I can't afford to live on the money I make as an adjunct."

Strong Answers:
Better answers to these questions include references to big financial sacrifices and the narrowness of academia. These are elements that anyone can understand, and citing them will shield you from slipping into a long, painful, and overly personal narrative.

- "Grad school was a great experience, but it just wasn't making any financial sense for me in the long term. I've decided to take the next step and bring my love of science and my lab research skills to industry."
- "I learned so much in graduate school, but academia is a narrow, small world. It seemed like we were just talking to ourselves and it was all so abstract. I've been volunteering for

political causes for more than a decade, including while I was in grad school, and now I've decided to devote myself to advocacy full-time. I want the work I do to have a bigger impact in the real world."

Should You Mention That You Might Go on the Market Again?

In short, no. It would be foolish for any employer to hire someone who says that she plans on leaving in a year; employers always lose money on training new employees. It's no different than telling an employer that you plan to leave in a year for any other reason. You would never say—or at least you'd never be hired if you did say—that you plan to leave in a few months to travel around the world, go to law school, move across the country, have a child, or stay home and work on a novel.

Many academics have difficulty saying that they're leaving academia; try to make some kind of peace with it before you get to this point of interviewing. Remember that taking a job outside the academy doesn't mean that you have to give up research, writing, and thinking. Besides, you don't know what will happen between now and next fall. Maybe you'll decide that you like your new lifestyle. Maybe there won't be any desirable jobs in your field. Maybe your tastes will change. You can't be sure. So why shoot yourself in the foot just to set yourself apart as someone with a "higher calling"?

What to say so you're not exactly lying:
- "I love college teaching, but the job market is really tight. I know that I can fulfill my love of teaching in other ways."
- "Graduate school was a once-in-a-lifetime opportunity, but I'm ready to roll up my sleeves and get some practical experience."

After the Interview

Now that you've survived the interview, you still can't wait around for the phone to ring. Your next task is to reiterate your interest in the position by sending a thank-you note. A brief, well-worded note sent promptly (within twenty-four hours of your interview) solidifies a good impression. As with cover letters, don't use a one-size-fits-all thank-you letter. Be specific but concise; follow up on a question you were asked in the interview, or mention a particular project within the company that interests you. E-mailing a thank-you note is standard practice, as snail mail can take too long. Don't spend too much time dwelling on the specifics though; it's better to send a brief, warm, sincere note promptly than none at all.

What If the Interview Doesn't Go Well?

One PhD went through all the steps listed above in order to interview at a company where she really wanted to work. She was prepared, confident, and ready to wow the employer with her editorial and project management skills. But five minutes into the interview, she "realized they were looking for a technical expert—not me at all."

After enduring an uncomfortable discussion about her limited technical abilities, she figured she had nothing to lose and decided to turn a negative into a positive. Within a few hours of the awkward meeting, she e-mailed her interviewers to let them know that while she sensed that she wasn't a good match for the particular position they had discussed, she was still enthusiastic about the company and had skills that would be an asset in other departments. The interviewer wrote back immediately and offered to set up an interview for her in another department that would be a better fit. Her forthrightness and her confidence in her own abilities earned her a good reference from her first interviewer, and she was offered the second job.

The Job Offer (or Lack Thereof)

First of all, be prepared for the possibility that all your hard work might not pay off. The good news about not being selected for a post-academic job is that, unlike in academia, you don't have to wait another year to mount a new search. So don't despair if an offer doesn't materialize. Instead, try to learn as much as possible from your experience. If you're comfortable with the idea, ask the interviewer to share their reasons for not selecting you; you may get valuable feedback.

If, however, your hard work does turn into an offer, resist the impulse to jump for joy and scream your immediate cries of acceptance over the phone. You may have years of student loans and mountains of credit card debt, but that's all the more reason to consider the offer carefully. The moment you say "yes," you've lost all your negotiating power. Express your pleasure and enthusiasm and clarify the terms of the offer. Ask the employer to send you a quick, informal e-mail bulleting out the basics of the offer so that you have something in writing, and ask for a few days to consider. Use this time to make sure this is the job you really want.

Negotiation

Once you've decided that this is the job for you, you still need to control your enthusiasm when talking with your future employer. Amada Sandoval, a graduate student in English who once worked in human resources for a large firm, told us that she was amazed at how few people, especially women, tried to negotiate their salaries. As part of her job, she offered people less than she was prepared to pay. "If they didn't speak up for themselves, they started at lower salaries than they would've had otherwise," she recalls. Academia certainly doesn't prepare you for these kind of negotiations. Professors' salaries are rarely open to much negotiation, even when the job market isn't tight. But you'll need to learn this skill as you enter the business world, because you can give yourself a $5,000 or $10,000 raise before you even begin work. And negotiating is so common, you'll actually look a little odd if you don't try to better your offer.

The tone of your negotiations should be friendly and constructive. You're trying to work out an agreeable arrangement with the company, not grandstanding or bluffing about your enormous value as an employee. Instead, you want to present options and then keep quiet while they're being considered.

Say nothing about salary or benefits until you have a job offer in writing.

It may take awhile for the company to produce a written offer (there's often lots of legalese involved), but be patient. Assure the manager that you're very interested in working together, and you look forward to talking more specifically about these issues once have something in writing. As mentioned above, an informal e-mail is just fine for this purpose.

Research appropriate salaries in the field.

"Graduate students simultaneously overestimate and underestimate their own worth," says John Romano, former English professor turned network television producer. "They think they could be the next Spielberg, but they don't believe me when I say it's possible to get an entry-level screenwriting job." We all suffer these wild swings of confidence. One minute you think that you deserve a vice president's salary, and the next minute you're sure you belong in the mailroom. The cure for this disease is simple: Do some research. There are numerous websites (including www .salary.com and the Bureau of Labor Statistics, www.bls.gov) that offer information on starting salaries for a variety of fields and positions. In addition, use your industry network to get a sense of what average salaries are for someone with your qualifications.

Let the employer throw out the first number.

If the employer gives you a salary range, focus on the higher number. You may, for example, want to say something like "[The higher figure] seems a little on the low side to me for what these positions typically pay, but I'm sure we can work something out."

And no matter what the employer says, remember to wait for the written offer before making a commitment.

Use objective criteria.

If you decide to ask for more money, be prepared to back up your request with specific reasons. It's not enough to just say, "I want more money." It's much better to provide data indicating that the offer on the table is below average for the position in question, or that you're considering a better offer from another company for a similar position. Your current salary is irrelevant, so don't reveal it.

Learn your benefits.

Salary isn't the only thing to negotiate when you accept a job offer. Maybe you want to adjust the start date or ask for additional vacation days for an already-planned trip. Also consider negotiating relocation expenses, flexible hours, tuition assistance for relevant classes, and so on. An employer may have limits on how much s/he can pay but could have more flexibility in these areas. For example, PhDs learn quickly that a six-month salary review (instead of twelve-month) is a smart request, and one that's easy for the employer to accommodate. If you're a graduate student, you may not have much experience with benefit packages, so be sure to analyze your written offer carefully. Ask friends about what their health and other benefit packages include and how your offer compares. Benefits can be as important as salary in determining your new quality of life. Your ability to negotiate your salary, your responsibilities, and your promotion path is never stronger than before you've accepted a job offer. Don't waste this opportunity.

Adjusting to Your New Job

Once you've accepted the position, take a deep breath and get ready for your next adventure. Be prepared for some anxiety, since any transition is stressful. But know that because you've been trained to learn, you have all the skills you need to handle being the new kid on the block. Josh Fost, a PhD in neurobiology who now works in consulting, remembers the shock of his first day: There was "no orientation whatsoever in the beginning; I was overwhelmed. I sat in my cube trying to be productive on a project I didn't have a clue about. I opened up the manuals, stared at the code, and three weeks later the project was done and massively successful." While his graduate school training helped him puzzle out a solution, Fost remembers feeling that he was no longer on familiar turf. He was using the same computer programs, doing similar kinds of work, but he was surrounded by an entirely different culture: "Suddenly, I'm wearing khakis!" he remembers.

A good rule to remember in your new job: Don't say or do anything rash for three months. Don't complain and don't make any suggestions. It will be tempting to propose all kinds of "improvements" to the way things work during your first few days and weeks on the job. However, resist the impulse to speak up. Wait until you have a better understanding of why things are done a certain way before you open your mouth. Concentrate on asking questions and learning how things work first. And even after a few months on the job, it's wise to phrase your suggestions as questions: "What's the logic behind X? Has anyone ever tried Y in the past?" Make sure your questions are sincere requests for information, rather than thinly veiled judgments. In time, you'll be able to make informed suggestions, and your colleagues will receive them much more readily now that you have proved yourself as a colleague.

Whatever bumps you encounter in your first job, remember that you've taken a first step into a new world. Few choices in life are perfect, irrevocable, or final. Give your new job a fair shot, but remember that if you don't like your first gig, you have the tools and the skills to make a change. You're not stuck for life. In fact, it's common practice outside academia to gradually refine your career path as you learn more about yourself and gain new experiences and perspectives.

....

POST-ACADEMIC PROFILE:
SCOTT KEETER, PHD IN POLITICAL SCIENCE, DIRECTOR
OF SURVEY RESEARCH, PEW RESEARCH CENTER FOR THE
PEOPLE & THE PRESS

Jobs at foundations or think tanks appeal to many academics because they seem to mimic the research you have been doing inside the academy—except with better pay, shorter vacations, and, one hopes, less virulent office politics. But as Scott Keeter can attest, the qualities and experiences that foundation and think-tank employers seek may be quite different from the ones acquired in a typical doctoral program.

Keeter successfully transitioned from a career as faculty member in political science to being chief methodologist at the Pew Research Center. Now that he's on the hiring side, he has advice for academics who want to make the switch.

Keeter was studying polling as a professor at Rutgers when a former faculty member who was managing NBC's exit-poll operation hired him to work as an analyst on election night. "That work, which involves poring through the mounds of data from the exit polls and very quickly writing stories for the on-air correspondents to read and discuss, introduced me to many senior polling professionals and journalists. It also helped me develop a feel for doing research that would be used not only by academics but by policy makers and journalists," he recalls.

Some might see the election night analyst job as a lucky break, but Keeter sees it as the result of good networking, an activity he has continued throughout his career and which eventually led to an introduction to Andrew Kohut, the former president of the Pew Research Center.

"The job-search process in the private and nonprofit sectors is usually quite different from the one used in academe. Jobs are often not as well publicized in the private and nonprofit world, which means that knowing where to look, or having contacts who let you know about opportunities, is more important," Keeter advises.

Academics who want to make the transition need to demonstrate in a cover letter and interview that they have the qualities foundations value. "In addition to many other qualities, we value experience in collaborative settings. It's important for a candidate to have had some kind of collaborative experience, which can be difficult to obtain as an academic since the dissertation experience itself is an isolating one. And it's even more isolating for top students who have fellowships as they tend to focus on their own work instead of interacting with others through teaching or other projects." Let your references know that prospective employers may ask about these qualities and prepare them to talk about more than just your doctoral research.

"It's also important that candidates be able to work at a faster pace than usually found in the academic world. In applied survey-research settings, we tend to have multiple projects under way at the same time," Keeter adds.

If you're interested in foundation work, Keeter encourages academics to get involved in relevant professional organizations, like AAPOR, the American Association for Public Opinion Research. Attending meetings is a great way to begin networking. Internships and part-time jobs are another "good way for students to get relevant experience in applied settings and develop a portfolio that can help get them noticed when seeking a consultant job or a full-time job outside of academe."

Conclusion

Although Carol Barash is an expert on women writers of the eighteenth century, one of her favorite books is a children's story called *The Big Step*. "It's a story—really a fairy tale—about a poor boy who wants to marry the king's daughter. The king says the boy can't marry the princess unless he can jump over the tallest tower in the kingdom," she recalls. The boy invents all sorts of devices to get over the tower—a ladder, a catapult, a lever, a pulley—and ends up discarding each one after it fails to work. When the boy sees his little dog climbing up a pile of discarded inventions, he realizes that he doesn't need to leap over the tower in a single bound—he just needs to take small steps.

"And that's what it's like to leave the academy," she says. The story illustrates her belief that when trying a new career, "there's nothing wrong with being wrong." Even a big misstep can start you in the right direction. "You just need to take the first step, and the next steps will all be easier," Barash adds. Ann Kirschner, an academic, entrepreneur, and author, echoes this advice, reminding job hunters that "it'll never be this hard again." Once you get your first post-academic job, "no one will ever question your ability to adapt to the business world."

Remember these alums' wise words as you begin your career exploration. Try to silence the little professor inside you who dreads being wrong. Television producer John Romano warns that the worst decisions are motivated by fear. Every choice has consequences, but they are rarely disastrous or irrevocable. He says, "Security can rule you. Security involves other risks. For most of us, we don't realize how low the stakes really are in our twenties. You go down a lot of wrong roads and still turn out okay." The best decisions, we say, are made from passion, desire, and excitement. Move toward what you love, rather than shrinking from what you fear.

Instead of worrying that you'll never find the perfect job, concentrate on building the life you want. What do you need to be happy? Where do you want to live? How do you want to spend your days? Would you like to learn something new? Do you want to return to something old? Try to take what you love about the academic world and leave the rest behind. As journalist and PhD Alex Pang reminded us, "The life of the mind is highly portable."

You probably feel that being a teacher and a scholar is a calling, that no other career will fill you in exactly the same way. But our goal has been to show you that there are other ways to arrange your life. You can make a life for yourself that is as good as, or even better than, the one that you hope to enjoy in academia.

It's no accident that all the people we've introduced to you in this book are happy and successful. Maybe you think we've stacked the deck by only telling you about people who enjoy the post-academic life. Maybe you're wondering if we've overlooked all the miserable former academics. We admit that we looked for people with interesting stories to share, but we didn't censor anyone.

So why did most of the people we interviewed seem to share the same positive view of their new careers? We think it's because their post-academic lives have been shaped by the same intelligence, the same creativity, and the same desire to learn that brought them to graduate school in the first place. Intellectuals don't lose their abilities the moment they step off campus. The talents that made you successful in academia can propel you into the post-academic world. Strong, independent thinkers can't help carving out interesting careers. Success is the almost inevitable side effect of pursuing what you love.

Even if you believe us when we say that your instincts and your passion are the best career guides you can find, what does that mean for you in practical terms? If it's all about serendipity and kismet, what on earth are you supposed to do today? Remember that we haven't suggested radical changes or abrupt shifts. Instead, we've tried to get you to examine your life more closely. So all you need to do today is consider taking some small half-steps into your own undiscovered future. As Cynthia Thomiszer described her move from English professor to computer company executive, "My decision to leave academia was more of an evolution than a revolution." And that's our goal: to sow the seeds of evolution among academics.

Finally, we want to caution you that there are no short cuts. It takes time, effort, and persistence to land your first job outside academia. But if you put in the work, you will be successful. "You have to keep trying," says Shaohua Zhou, a PhD in developmental and cell biology who now works in consulting for Gallup. "I would tell my friends: 'Don't tell me your university isn't prestigious enough. Don't tell me that you graduated too many years ago. Don't tell me you don't have time. If you keep looking, if you keep learning, in the end, you can find a job.' You have to be persistent, and that's a strength of graduate students."

We want to hear about your experiences. Tell us about your fears, your hopes, your mistakes, and your triumphs. Have we helped you? What did we forget to tell you? E-mail us at sowhatbook@ gmail.com and tell us your story. We'd love to hear from you.